The work of Pierre Jean Jouve (1887–197(
tor, influenced that of Pierre Emmanuel
David Gascoyne in England. In spiritual
all his previous writing. Renewing his
preoccupation with Freud (he married E   ̣ ̣ ̣ ̣ ̣ ̣ ̣ ̣ ̣ ̣a-
lyst, in 1925) and the mystics, he entered his 'vita nuova'. *Noces* (1928) and his
translations (with Pierre Klossowski), *Poèmes de la folie de Hölderlin* (1930),
preceded his most significant poetry collections: *Sueur de sang* (1935); *Matière
Céleste* (1937); *Kyrie* (1938). During that period, he established his reputation
as a novelist with *Paulina 1880* (1925), *Le Monde désert* (1927), *Hécate* (1928)
and *Vagadu* (1930), based on one of his wife's case histories, *Dans les années
profondes* (1932), and *La Scène capitale* (1935).

At fifteen, David Gascoyne (1916–2001) was translating Baudelaire,
Mallarmé, and Rimbaud – the dominating influence of his adolescence.
After the publication of the precocious *Roman Balcony and other poems*
(1932), and *Opening Day* the next year when he made his first visit to Paris,
the exciting discovery there of the poetry and novels of Pierre Jean Jouve in
1937 lead to the beginning of a life-long friendship with the writer
and his wife (Gascoyne underwent analysis with her), and proved a signifi-
cant turning point. *Hölderlin's Madness* (1938) represented his response to
Jouve's *Poèmes de la folie de Hölderlin*, and in *Poems 1937–42* (1943) Gascoyne
found his mature voice. He continued to translate the work of Jouve and of
contemporary French poets for the next fifty years.

Enitharmon Press have published many of his recent books, including
The Sun at Midnight (1970), *Paris Journal* (1978), *Journal 1936–37* (1980), *Selected
Poems* (1994), *Selected Verse Translations* (1996), *Selected Prose 1934–1996* (1998)
and the novella *April* (2000).

Roger Scott taught for thirty years at a Northumbrian comprehensive
school, as Head of Spanish then of English. From 1993 he lectured part-time
at Northumbria University while researching for his doctorate: 'David
Gascoyne: From Darkness into Light. A Study of his Poetry 1932–1950.' He
has edited several of the Gascoyne texts published by Enitharmon, and
contributed to *Modern Poetry in Translation* and *Temenos Academy Review*. The
New Oxford Dictionary of National Biography (2004; 2005) includes his entries
on Roger Roughton and David Gascoyne. At present Scott is collating
Gascoyne's unpublished and uncollected work and compiling a bibliogra-
phy of Kathleen Raine's poetry and prose. He is a Visiting Research Fellow
at Northumbria University.

Despair Has Wings

Selected Poems
of Pierre Jean Jouve

Translated by David Gascoyne

Edited with an introductory essay
by Roger Scott

ENITHARMON PRESS

First published in 2007
by Enitharmon Press
26B Caversham Road
London NW5 2DU

www.enitharmon.co.uk

Distributed in the UK by
Central Books
99 Wallis Road
London E9 5LN

Distributed in the USA and Canada
by Dufour Editions Inc.
PO Box 7, Chester Springs
PA 19425, USA

ISBN: 978-1-904634-40-9

Enitharmon Press gratefully acknowledges the financial support of
Arts Council England, London.

British Library Cataloguing-in-Publication Data.
A catalogue record for this book is available
from the British Library.

Designed by Libanus Press
and printed in England by
Antony Rowe Ltd

I remember I was there
When fire-bombs slashed the street
I sat on the stair
Beneath your feet
Two babies in my arms
And you read Baudelaire.

As the flames leapt
And people ran with water
I clutched my daughter
And son, and wept.
You said: 'Le désespoir a des ailes
L'amour a pour aile nacré
Le désespoir
Les sociétés peuvent changer.'
You quoted Jouve.
We did not move
Until it was all quiet
And we found we were not dead.

ELIZABETH SMART: from
   'To David Gascoyne, On his Sixty-Fifth Birthday'

'The abyss is our element. Flung into it […] we sprout wings.'
LÉON CHESTOV

CONTENTS

SECTION TWO:

APPENDIX A

APPENDIX B

ACKNOWLEDGEMENTS

I would like to record my deep gratitude for the friendship, unfailing help, kindness and encouragement shown throughout the making of this book by Judy Gascoyne, Michael Hamburger, Allan Ingram, Kaye Kossick, Margaret Callander, Jeremy Reed, Alan Munton, Anthony Astbury, Anthony Rudolf, Michel Rémy, Michèle Duclos, Yves Bonnefoy, and the late Alan Clodd, Kathleen Raine and Yves de Bayser. Stephen Stuart-Smith's gentle guidance and sympathetic understanding, as always, have been crucial.

I am indebted, too, to Sally Brown and Chris Fletcher in the British Library Manuscripts Department; to Erin O'Neill at the BBC Written Archives Centre; to Melissa Burkhart, Ruth Carruth at the McFarlin Library, University of Tulsa; to Vincent Giroud, Timothy Young, Kevin Repp and Becca Lloyd of the Beinecke Rare Book and Manuscript Library of Yale University. Their patient and friendly response to my numerous queries and requests has been of immense value.

My thanks, too, to Sebastian Barker for permission to quote stanzas three and four of his mother's poem, 'To David Gascoyne, On his Sixty-Fifth Birthday'.

And finally, for their constant support, interest and involvement, my especial thanks to my wife, Pat, our daughter Kate, and son Mark for his technical expertise and advice.

NOTE

I have transcribed David Gascoyne's unpublished versions of Jouve's poems from various manuscript notebooks. They are drafts only, and in the main are unrevised by him. Editorial conjectures are indicated with a question mark or included inside square brackets in italics.

DESPAIR HAS WINGS

David Gascoyne & Pierre Jean Jouve

'A poet I still regard as the greatest it has been my good fortune to know'[1]

In an article published in *Le Monde* in 1984, Hubert Juin ranks influences on David Gascoyne as follows:

> Gascoyne has his masters. At the very top: Rimbaud and Hölderlin. And just below that: Pierre Jean Jouve. He has a guru: Jacob Boehme. He found guides, very uncomfortable ones, it's true: Kierkegaard, Chestov, Fondane, Berdiaev.[2]

In the entry for 27 February–1 March 1940 in his *Collected Journals 1936–1942*, Gascoyne lists the literary figures who have influenced and inspired him to a marked extent: he names Rimbaud, Pascal, Marx and Freud, Breton and Fondane; then makes particular reference to Jouve: 'to a great extent' and to Blanche Reverchon-Jouve: 'quite as much'. In the 'Afterword', completed in November 1989, he writes: 'Among the writers I was lucky enough to have frequented in Paris before the War, Pierre Jean Jouve and Benjamin Fondane both had a decisive and lasting influence on me.'[3]

Five years earlier in an interview for another French newspaper, he had agreed with Patrick Mauries that Blanche Reverchon was just as important to him as her husband in his life and development as a writer. At the same time, he acknowledged that Pierre Jean Jouve does not appear often in the *Collected Journals*: 'If you're keeping a journal, you can't know in advance and select what will be truly important for you afterwards.'[4]

*

The year 1937 was crucial in David Gascoyne's development which saw a marked change in his poetry and personal philosophy. He had gone to Paris to live for two years in an attic overlooking Notre Dame. In the autumn, quite providentially, he found a copy of Jouve's *Poèmes de la folie de Hölderlin* (1930)[5] in a second-hand bookseller's box on the *quais*. This translation from the German 'led to my essay, poems and translations[6] published by Dent the following year as *Hölderlin's Madness*.'[7] He explains in an article published in 1981 that 'I had thus discovered a poet whose work, which at that time was far from being complete, suddenly seemed to present an ideal example of the kind of poetry that I would have wished to write then.'[8] Then he bought *Les Noces* (1931) and various novels – everything that Jouve had written in poetry and prose – from a bookshop beside the Gare du Luxembourg, and opposite the Luxembourg Gardens. Noting his interest – Gascoyne had just been reading *Histoires sanglantes* and *Hécate* – the owner introduced Gascoyne to Jouve who was both a relative of hers and a regular weekly customer, which led to an invitation to visit the apartment at 8 rue de Tournon, a 'mixture of luxuriousness and austerity [...] and silent. I have always thought that this house was that described by Henry James in his novel *The Ambassadors*.' Instead of wallpaper there were paintings by Sima and two 'extraordinary'[9] works by Balthus: *Alice*,[10] in Jouve's bedroom, and the picture of a young girl asleep in a green mountain meadow illustrating one of his poems.[11]

A short while afterwards, Jouve and his second wife, Blanche Reverchon, his senior by nine years,[12] asked Gascoyne to their Thursday *soirées*, attended from 9 p.m. to midnight by writers, philosophers, musicians and some of Blanche's most interesting patients, like Schiaparelli and Gascoyne himself.[13] Blanche, in collaboration with Jouve and Bernard Groethuysen, had published with Gallimard in 1923 their translation, *Trois Essais sur la théorie sexuelle de Freud*.[14] In March 1933, Jouve and his wife had collaborated on an article for *La Nouvelle Revue Française*, 'Moments d'une Psychanalyse'[15] which, according to Margaret Callander, 'describes the mental illness of a young woman, and transcribes the most rich and suggestive of her strange dreams.' She points out that Jouve 'used this or very similar material' in one of his *Histoires sanglantes* (1932), 'Les Rois Russes.'[16] In fact, Madame Jouve, who had been analysed by Freud,[17] supplied her husband with a mass of psychiatric material which he incorporated in the poems of his collection *Sueur de sang* and in his novel, *Aventure de Catherine Crachat*, which Gascoyne considers to be 'the most remarkable ever written on psycho-analysis.'[18] He always believed that 'Jouve's debt to her [Blanche] was generally very greatly underestimated.'[19] Jean Wahl wrote that 'Blanche Jouve was for Jouve what Beatrice represented for Dante.'[20]

Jouve's 'real career as a poet began, according to him,' writes Germaine Brée, 'with a double conversion to Christianity and to psychoanalysis.'[21] Ian Higgins argues that Jouve was recognized as a poet in 1933 with *Sueur de sang*, 'in which his interest in the Freudian theory of the unconscious combines with his Catholic spirituality in a search for release from the sense of imperfection attaching to bodily life.'[22] Referring to Jouve's 'flexible appropriation of psychoanalysis,' Mary Lewis Shaw has indicated that he 'manages to integrate very pointed aspects of Freud's psychoanalytic theory into his poetic world, even as he builds its themes and structure around Catholic imagery and doctrine;'[23] but Shaw goes further, suggesting that 'even poems adhering to "traditional" religious doctrine can subvert the parallels and connections they set forth between poetry and the word of God.'[24]

*

Jouve saw the writer's task as 'the unceasing transformation of personal matter,' explains Gascoyne:

> His objectivization of his personal experience – both of the vicissitudes of sexuality and of the spirit's wrestling for faith – often took the form in his poetry of an approximation to musical composition. The poems consist largely of inventions, of suites and of variations on themes, and one of the forms of 'personal matter' transformed by Jouve in this way resulted from an exceptionally acute response to the power of music. A frequenter from the inception of the Salzburg festivals, an admirer and friend of Bruno Walter, Jouve found inspiration for poems above all in the works of Mozart and Alban Berg.[25]

Between 1935 and 1939, Jouve was the music critic of *La Nouvelle Revue Française*, and on one occasion was given tickets by the composer and his wife for the first performance in France of Béla Bartók's *Suite for Two Pianos and Percussion*. Gascoyne was one of the few people asked to accompany Jouve. After the concert, Bartók returned with them to the rue de Tournon apartment. For the rest of the evening, Bartók – 'very reserved and hardly speaking French – returned many times to the Jouves' grand piano to play pieces from his 'Mikrokosmos' series which he had then only just completed.[26] He seemed at home,' Gascoyne recalled, 'realizing that Jouve truly appreciated his music, then still reputed to be impossibly dissonant and rebarbative. Rare and unforgettable occasion!'[27] In his capacity as music critic, Jouve wrote on Mozart and Alban Berg, as well as Bartok.[28] Gascoyne's translation of one of these essays, 'La grandeur actuelle de Mozart', appeared in *Horizon* in 1940 as 'The Present Greatness of Mozart'.[29] He writes:

> It was to this essay that I owe my first mature appreciation of the true significance and exceptional greatness of Mozart, as like so many supposedly musical people in the thirties, my idea of his music was very much the conventional one, in which the aspect of sunny charm and the pathos of prematurely carried-off genius combined to hide the profundity and sublimity that characterize the true Mozart. [...] I know very well I could never hope to approach the quality of understanding and the beauty and aptness of language that Pierre Jean Jouve achieved whenever he wrote about music.[30]

Gascoyne's poem, 'Mozart: Sursum Corda'[31] sets 'supernal voices' in the 'sostenuto of the sky' against 'mortal deafness', and ends with these beautiful lines corresponding to the imagery of the Metaphysical poets:

> Beyond our speech
> To tell what equinoxes of the infinite
> The spirit ranges in its rare utmost flight.

It is difficult not to see here an echo of Jouve's own poem, 'Mozart', in *Les Noces*.[32]

> One reason perhaps why I always felt a particularly strong affinity with Jouve is that I had a musical education myself (as a Cathedral chorister) and early developed a passionate interest in contemporary music. Before meeting or even having heard of Jouve I had attended the first

English concert performance of Berg's Wozzeck in the old Queen's Hall [...]. After the war I was glad to be able to take with me on a visit to the [Jouves'] rue Antoine-Chantin apartment a then new recording of Berg's concert aria *Der Wein* (setting of Stefan George's translation from Baudelaire). Jouve had never heard it before listening to it on his record-player.[33]

Gascoyne always believed that one of the strongest links in his friendship with Jouve was their admiration for Mozart and Bartók but, more particularly, their shared passion for Berg. Shortly after the latter's death in 1935, Gascoyne had written two drafts of the 'Elegiac Stanzas in Memory of Alban Berg' which he considered 'unsatisfactory' in English.[34] The long poem was rewritten in French in 1939 after his return to his parents' home in England, as *Strophes Elégiaques à la mémoire d'Alban Berg*.[35] Why Gascoyne chose to return to the abandoned project some three years later and then composed the long poem in French is difficult now to ascertain. When I put this question to him on his eighty-fifth birthday in 2001 he answered straight away: 'Because there were things that I wanted to say in French at that time.'[36] The poet, translator and essayist Michael Hamburger offered a most perceptive observation touching on this question in a letter he wrote to me on 22 February 2002. Hamburger suggests that in Gascoyne's case the struggle 'to incorporate the whole of a truth in poems [...] was exacerbated by the pull between French and English exemplars. [...] In his English poems there was a tension between traditional rhetoric (and rhythms and metres) and the colloquialism established by his immediate predecessors, Auden and the rest. Although Verlaine thought he wrung the neck of rhetoric in French the rhetoric re-asserted itself even in Surrealism and all the other modernisms. [...] Somehow French is a more abstract language than English; therefore perhaps more congenial to David in his search for transcendent spirituality.'[37]

In a searching and illuminating essay, 'Tombeau du musicien. Les poèmes de Pierre Jean Jouve et de David Gascoyne sur Alban Berg', Jean-Yves Masson argues that 'the question of the superiority of poetry to music, or of music to poetry, preoccupied [...] Gascoyne for whom music and poetry were always two complementary expressions of the absolute thirst which lies at the heart of the human condition [my translation].' He goes on to discuss the examples of the Orpheus figure in *Hölderlin's Madness* and the angelic voices in the poem 'Concert of Angels'. Masson contends that Gascoyne 'needed to use the French language in his "Strophes élégiaques à la mémoire d'Alban Berg" to explain what Berg's work signified for him: perhaps he wished to articulate clearly, by distancing it, this rapport with History which, expressed in English, would have been too didactic [my translation].' [38]

Jouve devoted a poem to Berg in his collection *La Vierge de Paris* (Fribourg, 1944; Paris, 1946), [39] and dedicated his collection *Langue* (1952) 'to the spirit of Alban Berg'; [40] in 1953 he published with the musicologist Michel Fanu a study of Berg's opera *Wozzeck*. [41] One section of *Mélodrame* (1957) is entitled 'Tombeau de Berg' / 'Berg's Tomb', in three parts. In one of his 1950 notebooks, Gascoyne began to translate an essay by Jouve on Berg's *Violin Concerto*. [42] In another from that decade, various entries point to his concern to engage with the persona and role of Lulu in *Wozzeck*, beginning with an incomplete summary of the plot of Berg's opera. Gascoyne amused himself by making a note in a 'Commonplace Notebook' dated 1948:

> The connection with Stravinsky is striking, but seems to have struck no-one but me – I should think Pierre would repudiate it with colère and irritation – but 'Noces' – 'Symphonie à Dieu' – the 'Porche' and S's 'Mass', – 'Gloire', is not this one of the essential elements of S's aesthetic ideal 'to the greater glory of God' – the super-human light that breaks through in the golden clanging at the end of 'Les Noces', for instance? Compare their photographs also. [Compare the photographs of Bartók and Klee]. [43]

*

By 1938, there is a 'renewal of vision' [44] with the attendant change of sensibility in Gascoyne's approach to poetry, now centred on the conscious and the metaphysical rather than on the un-/sub-conscious and the illogic of the practising Surrealist he no longer wished to be. He observed many years later that although Jouve was not a member of the

Surrealist group in France, 'there was a connection that he too [like them] used the unconscious as a source of poetry.'[45]

> One of the most characteristic features of Pierre Jean Jouve as a novelist and as a poet has always been his highly developed awareness of the Unconscious, of the guilt by which the Unconscious is dominated in all men, and of the struggle in the Unconscious of the instincts of life and death, which always seem to be locked inextricably together. Poetry, like the works of the great mystics, Jouve regards as proceeding from Eros, or rather, as representing the highest degree of sublimation of the erotic instinct [...].[46]

Jouve himself wrote retrospectively in *En Miroir* that after rejecting all his early work up to 1925, he was seeking 'for an order that was my own. Beyond the defined instinctive structures [...] one must be able to imagine the existence of an area of images which I called the poetic unconscious, the area that generates and holds together the inspiration within the two main fundamental schemes of Eros and Death.'[47]

Three of Jouve's poems: 'Gravida', 'Sur la Pente', 'La Bouche d'ombre', were published in the Surrealist periodical, *Minotaure*, No. 6 (Winter, 1935). Gascoyne told Lucien Jenkins that 'Jouve uses the material that the Surrealists used. His poetic art is the cultivation of spontaneity to obtain contact with the unconscious.' He added, 'He would not have known what he was going to write when he sat down to write.'[48] An unpublished 'Note' in one of Gascoyne's notebooks dating from the early 1950s, now in the McFarlin Library at the University of Tulsa, took this last point further:

> Jouve cannot always recognize himself speaking in what he has written. Another voice, the Other voice, ventriloquizes through him. He is capable of allowing the subliminal message to inscribe itself at the heart of his poetry in this way, because of the long, utterly disinterested toil which he has devoted to the perfecting of a technique of imaginatively transcendental discursivity (his intention meanwhile often seeming preoccupied with private aesthetic-erotic autosatisfaction).[49]

Gascoyne stresses, however, the importance for him that 'at the same time there was [in Jouve] a spiritual dimension lacking in Surrealist poetry.'[50] He comments: 'the Surrealists, of course, hardly appreciated the mystical[51] Christian element expressed [by Jouve] in *Le Paradis perdu* and *Les Noces*, intensified in all his work after *Sueur de sang*.'[52] Quoting Jouve, Gascoyne explains that one of the basic aims of his poetry was 'to arrive at a poetic language which justifies itself completely as song, and to find a religious perspective in the poetic act, – the only response to the nothingness of time.'[53] But he acknowledges that, though brought up as a Catholic, the French writer 'escapes all easy categorization as a religious poet', recognizing in himself a 'residual puritanism' and being referred to by one of his critics as 'Jansenist'.[54]

Jouve's Catholicism (aside from his interest in Freud) which is expressed in terms of that 'mystical religious tendency'[55] [the influence St Teresa of Avila and St John of the Cross], may well have opened up for Gascoyne a new route from Surrealism to, at least, a broad Christianity, and the growing belief that the acute and frightening awareness of the void, foregrounded so frequently and unequivocally in the *Collected Journals 1936–1942*, could only be countered by religious faith.[56] Jean Starobinski, Jouve scholar and explorer of psychoanalysis and literature, points out that 'the image of the interior void [...] is repeated and revived as an integral part of the preface to *Sueur de sang*.'[57]

If Hölderlin 'found his own poetic voice when he met Susette [Gontard],[58] as David Constantine suggests, then Gascoyne began to find his when he discovered Jouve's translations of the German poet and met Jouve himself.[59] In *Hölderlin's Madness* (1938) Gascoyne provided versions of twenty-two poems from Jouve and Klossowski's *Poèmes de la Folie de Hölderlin*.[60] There is a clear affinity between Gascoyne and Hölderlin in their double vision: the conflation of both private and external worlds in their poetry. Francis Scarfe reviewed *Hölderlin's Madness* in *Twentieth Century Verse*, welcoming the publication: 'In revealing us Hölderlin, Mr Gascoyne has done his generation a service.'[61] *The Criterion* reviewer found that '[...] in submitting himself to Hölderlin's vision he [Gascoyne] has achieved a clearness and a wholeness that he never reached in his first book.'[62] Derek Stanford referred specifically to the use Gascoyne had made of Jouve's versions, which 'meant that the impact of the German poet was modified by two translations: a feature which would lead us to expect a certain anaemic quality in the work. Nothing, however, is farther from the truth: power of image, clarity of language, and simplicity of music characterize the verse [...].'[63]

Gascoyne interpolated four original poems in *Hölderlin's Madness*: 'Figure in a Landscape', 'Orpheus in the Underworld', 'Tenebrae' and 'Epilogue'. The influence of Jouve's 'mystical religious intensity'[64] is unmistakable in 'Tenebrae', a luminous poem charged with tension and feeling, and concern for the human condition. The central figure in each of the four poems is a composite of Hölderlin-Gascoyne, but with the addition in 'Epilogue' of the supremely suffering Orpheus,[65] imprisoned in his own madness. At the end of his introductory essay to *Hölderlin's Madness*, Gascoyne writes emphatically: 'His poetry is stronger than despair and reaches into the future and the light.' However, Michel Rémy rightly points to the underlying problem: 'the mystery for Hölderlin of the Gods' distance, and for Gascoyne and Jouve the mystery of God's absence.'[66]

Gascoyne has described how, by 17 October 1938 after the Munich crisis, he had lapsed into a terrible state of depression and inertia: 'complete paralysis, surrounded by walls entirely black as in a dungeon.'[67] At 2 a.m. he decided to go to see Mme Jouve who told him: 'I can't perhaps make you better but I can certainly help you a little.'[68] Analysis began shortly afterwards on 22 October. On 27 October he got up at ten o'clock and 'went out to analysis at eleven.' Later that day, he was writing in his journal in the Café Rotonde: 'Rather a difficult session today: tried to talk about a scene in a film [...] Also talked about my "subterranean" fantasies. Ended up by describing a little dream which I thought was quite uninteresting but which apparently is simply fraught with significance.'[69] He saw her every two days and had the fullest confidence in her.[70] On 29 October he recorded: 'Miserably restless night. Went out to analysis late and unshaven, with a thick cold in the head. Difficult and inarticulate hour with Mme. Jouve. Too worried by the money situation to be able to talk much.'[71] Recording on 31 October the course of his analysis with Blanche, Gascoyne wrote:

At present I have no clear idea of what is happening; today brought out what seemed only a muddled collection of images. Talked about the intermittent bursts of creative enthusiasm I have, which so often fall flat because I feel incapable of fulfilling them. '"*La mariée est trop belle*", as the proverb says,' Mme. Jouve remarked.[72]

Gascoyne recalled in 1992: 'I have never forgotten this sentence, because it harbours the fundamental explanation of my problems.'[73] His analyst had told him that he had 'an exceptional faculty of transformation', and he supposed that included 'a particular aptitude for sublimating sex urges.'[74] On 3 November 1938, he wrote: 'My unconscious appears to have a very hostile opinion of Mme. Jouve, representing her as a witch with a pointed hat, a beard and horns! I am too polite, of course, to tell her so to her face.'[75] Four days later [7 November] he confided: 'Have got the jitters again today. Holding on by my teeth. Can see the future only as a black and bottomless pit. If it weren't for analysis I positively shouldn't be able to go on any longer' (p. 211). On 9 November Gascoyne reported:

> Mme. Jouve said yesterday that I was living through again at present a childhood nightmare. It certainly seems that I have been living in an abnormal state for some while past. The sense of suspense and unrelenting strain, the exaggerated proportions of small events, the violent inner ups and downs, all belong to nightmare rather than to everyday life.

The following evening, 'an important session' with Mme. Jouve suggested that they were 'beginning to get at things now. Apparently my censor is on too low a level, my aggressivity is too repressed, and I have a masochistic attitude towards my father, whom I imagine to be punishing me all the time' (p. 213). But progress was slow and a negative note was registered in the entry for 16 November:

> Have reached the sort of check in analysis as I am accustomed to meeting in my life. Feeling that there is a barrier between my conscious mind and the part that is being analysed. Lay on the couch this evening associating words and images *around something that was hidden* and which I could not get at. Then silence. '*Est-ce que ce n'est pas l'orgeuil qui vous empêche de parler?*'[76] demanded Mme. Jouve (p. 219).

On the last day of the year Gascoyne had been reading a book by an unnamed Viennese psychiatrist on *Character and Physique*, from which he deduced the fact that he belonged to the 'cyclothymic schizoid' group. 'I wonder,' he wrote, 'whether Mme. Jouve can ever really cure this? I suppose not. She can probably only diminish the worst effects' (31 December 1938, p. 235).

By 13 January 1939 Mme Jouve saw him daily after he had missed a session during what had been another difficult time. 'It's going better at present,' he recorded; but then surprisingly, on 22 January, he stated matter-of-factly that he had finished with analysis.[77] An interesting entry in *The Sun at Midnight* (1970) engages with the issue of illness, more particularly with Gascoyne's own mental problems, and relates specifically to Blanche Jouve's diagnosis, though she is not named:

> There is a sure and certain cure to all human maladies. Physician, cure thyself, is said to Everyone. This is possible. I know. My own psychoanalyst told me long ago that my chief trouble was to be diagnosed as an obsession with the old French adage: '*La mariée est trop belle*' [my emphasis]. It has taken me about thirty-one years to realize and understand how wise and true this was. My analyst, needless to say, is a woman.[78]

On 23 January, 1939 he received from Jouve a copy of his new collection, *Kyrie*[79], which he read with excited admiration:

> There was something miraculous in his being able to create poetry so intense and pure at a time like this [...]. Few writers' work could at first sight appear so remote from the world of politics, yet few poets have so profoundly suffered the events of current history, Czechoslovakia, Austria, Spain [...].[80]

In August, six months out of analysis, Gascoyne was agonizing again over the demands of his work: 'Alas! I cannot help being seriously worried by the flagrantly *schizophrenic* aspect of the whole business [of writing] – an aspect of which I am only too well aware. *Should like to consult Mme Jouve about this* [...] [my emphases] 22.VIII.39.'[81]

Two days later, the uncontrollable tension in Europe and within Gascoyne himself was mounting unbearably:

> 24.VIII.39. Beastly, bloody nightmare of a world. Another crisis. We're

in for it now [...] Something's *got* to happen. I don't mean only the war. I've got to get away soon, somewhere. *Must write to Blanche Jouve* [my emphasis]. Make a lot of effort, I'm becoming gradually more and more dotty, fanatical, otherworldly (p. 258).

*

Since their first meeting, Gascoyne had begun translating poems by Jouve, and they appeared before, during and after the war in various periodicals: *Delta*, No. 1 (Easter 1939), *Folios of New Writing* (Spring 1940), *Poetry* (London), No. 5 (March–April 1941), *Kingdom Come*, Vol. 3, No. 9 (November–December 1941), *New Directions 7* (1942), *New Road* 4 (April 1946), *Poetry* (London), No. 11 (September–October 1947). It is fascinating to examine the surprising number of revisions, probably because of the complexity of the original French poem. In addition, 'The Two Witnesses' shows significant modifications, mainly to his choice of adjectives and adjectival phrases.[82]

In addition to Jouve's essay on Mozart in *Horizon* (1940), Gascoyne's translation of the 'avant-propos' [preface] to *Sueur de sang*, 'Inconscient, spiritualité et catastrophe' / 'The Unconscious, Spirituality, Catastrophe', appeared in *Poetry* (London), Vol. 1, No. 4 (1941).[83] He had written to its editor, Tambimuttu, in 1940:

Dear Tambi,
I have the pleasure of sending you a translation I have just done of an essay of Jouve's which seems to me to be very much up your present street. I very much hope that you will like it well enough, and find it sufficiently relevant to the ideas you are now engaged in putting across, to include it in your next number. It's an essay I've vaguely been meaning to translate ever since I first read it about three years ago – at which time it helped me considerably to clarify several problems which were then bothering me about my own writing –; and then, after our last conversation about possible material for *Poetry*, it suddenly occurred to me that it was probably just the sort of thing you wanted, and I sat down and started the English version right away. (If the style seems a bit heavily baroque, I must explain that, if anything, the original French is more so; though personally, I don't like it any the less for that).[84]

In the same issue of *Poetry* (London), Tambimuttu devoted the whole of his prefatory 'Fourth Letter' to an enthusiastic welcome for Gascoyne's translation and examined Jouve's essay in some detail: 'In this number we publish an important statement by Pierre Jean Jouve,' he wrote, 'on poets, poetry, and the nature of creative thought, in the light of modern psychology and "meta-psychology". Thank you, David, for placing it at my disposal.'[85] In the list of contributors on the inside rear cover, Pierre Jean Jouve is that 'well-known French poet, known in England chiefly through the efforts of his friend and translator, David Gascoyne.'

In a notebook dating from that same year, Gascoyne planned the following publication: 'Pierre Jean Jouve: Selected Verse and Prose, translated into English by David Gascoyne'. There were to be seven sections:[86]
Introduction: biographical and critical essay (5,000 words);
Selected poems (about 20/30) with French text;
'The Present Greatness of Mozart';
'The Unconscious, Spirituality, Catastrophe';
Preface to *Histoires sanglantes;*
A short tale (('Le Château' or *Dans les années profondes*);
Prose piece published in *Fontaine.*[87]

Section II of *Poems 1937–42*, classified by Gascoyne as 'Metaphysical (or 'metapsychological'),[88] included five translations from Jouve's *Matière céleste* (1937) and *Kyrie*.[89] There is a pattern to the diction of Gascoyne's own poems here: 'mountains', 'peaks', 'rock' and 'valley', are set against 'desert', 'plain', 'fields', and both against 'sky/skies', 'cloud', 'moon', 'star(s)', so that at times there is a definite cosmic element. Glyn Pursglove refers perceptively to 'the astronomical infinities of the spirit's range' as one of 'the recurrent symbols in Gascoyne's poetic language.'[90] 'Light', 'sun(light)' are opposed by 'night', 'dark', 'black(ness)', 'fire' and 'red' are balanced by 'ice', and the world of the spirit with that of 'flesh' and 'blood'; Daniel E. Rivas points to Jouve's concern to 'harmonize' antinomies in his own poems.[91] 'Pain', 'grief' and 'anguish' resonate throughout this section of Gascoyne's *Poems 1937–42*, where the void or abyss is ever present, associated but not synonymous with 'hell', 'descent' and 'depths'. In Jouve's own collection of poems, 1939–1944, *La Vierge de Paris*, his 'Nuit des Saints' includes the line: 'Nous avons entendu le discours de l'abîme / Nous avons écouté ses premiers mots de sort /

Funeste et avons vu les anges sur la ville / Nous lui devons notre mort très farouche / Et ce n'est rien encore' / 'We have listened to the abyss's discourse / We have heard its first words of grievous fate / And have seen the angels above the city / We owe them our savage death / And it is nothing yet.'[92]

*

The poet Thomas Blackburn is struck by the 'lurid glare and sense of apocalyptic revelation' in Gascoyne's 'Metaphysical' poems.[93] In the second half of the 1930s there were clear indications of an apocalyptic finale to the decade in the rapidly deteriorating political situation in Europe with the rise of the fascist dictators and the horrors of the Civil War in Spain. And England in 1940–41, especially London, confronted a real apocalypse: systematic bombing and a threatened invasion by Hitler. The *Times Literary Supplement* reviewer of *Poems 1937–42* suggests that Gascoyne's volume might well indeed have been called 'Inferno'.[94]

Gascoyne himself had noted of Jouve in 1938: 'I know of no one who has so fully expressed the *apocalyptic* atmosphere of our time or with so strong an accent of the "sublime".'[95] Callander considers that the French writer had developed 'his apprehension of the triumph of the self-destructive elements in European civilization, until in *Kyrie* the conviction bursts forth in apocalyptic and prophetic language.'[96] The connection here with Gascoyne is strong. It would be difficult to disagree with Stephen Romer's contention that there is a marked sense of the apocalyptic in regard to the imagery, tone and content of several of the poems and journal entries from 1938 onwards.[97] Both poets pursue a burning spiritual quest for renewal; their role was to testify to the truth at a time of national danger. For Jouve, 'the creator of living values (the poet) must be against catastrophe.'[98] Callander states that when Jouve referred to a 'catastrophe' he did so 'by adopting Freud's method and diagnosing the spiritual diseases of our age as though psychoanalyzing an individual.'[99] According to Gascoyne, who extends her argument, Jouve's essay, 'Inconscient, spiritualité et catastrophe', amounts to a manifesto announcing the kind of poetry that had emerged from a full awareness of the unconscious mind as conceived by Freud,[100] and of its relation to both the basest and most sublime levels of the human psyche.[101] In Jean Starobinski's view, the preface to *Sueur de sang* 'testifies to the poet's interest in psychoanalytic discovery, but it isn't by any means an act of allegiance [...]'; he goes on to emphasize that Jouve sought 'to establish similarities between the primitive material of poetic work and the interior universe described through psychoanalysis.'[102] The opening couplet of *Sueur de sang* sheds light both on this underlying dualism and on the fascinating pair of novels [*Hécate* and *Vagadu*].'[103] Jouve had been engaged in writing: 'Les crachats sur l'asphalte m'ont toujours fait penser / A la face imprimée au voile des saintes femmes.' [104]

Jouve's message in 'The Unconscious, Spirituality, Catastrophe' was an urgent one:

> At this very hour, civilization is faced with the possibility of the direst of catastrophes; a catastrophe all the more menacing in that its first and last cause lies within man's own inner depths, mysterious in their action and governed by an independent logic; moreover, man is now as never before aware of the pulse of Death within him. The psycho-neurosis of the world has reached so advanced a stage that we can but fear the possibility of an act of suicide. Human society is reminded of the condition in which it found itself in the time of St John, or round the year 1000; it awaits the end, hoping it will come soon.[105]

And he employs heightened language in his reference to the Book of Revelation and medieval visions of the apocalypse:

> [...] we find ourselves heavy laden with the accumulated weight of instruments of Destruction; the noisome iniquities of its nations make of Europe 'the great harlot ... seated upon a scarlet coloured beast, full of names of blasphemy, having seven heads and ten horns...' (p. 114).[106]

While Jouve alone[107] made clear references to the demonology of the Antichrist and the associated beasts in a number of poems, both he and Gascoyne balanced the destructive and the redemptive elements of Apocalypse in the Book of Revelation.[108] In a 'post-face' [afterword] to *Les Témoins: poèmes choisis de 1930 à 1942* (1943), Jouve explains that 'the poems in this anthology have been chosen as "witnesses", that is to say, according to their relationship with the catastrophic, or strictly speaking, apocalyptic event of the War.'[109] That same year he wrote a preface, 'Poésie et catastrophe', to Pierre Emmanuel's *La Colombe*:

> Within, yet in opposition to the catastrophe, the poet represents that which is most permanent and sacred in all political action. His ultimate seriousness is surpassed only by that of the man who fights and puts his life at risk . [...] The true poet, the poet of the essential, draws on the forces of the soul and renders them in an eternal act, and thanks to that very act, engages with his times, engages with events [...].
> The poet is the only one who can possess the body and soul of truth; he is the only [...] one whose task it is to revive the deep instincts of love in opposition to the seductive instincts of death.[110]

Callander argues that 'If we except the work of Pierre Emmanuel, who acknowledges himself to have been directly influenced by Jouve himself [in *Qui est cet homme?*] we may say that Jouve is unusual in his adherence to and adaptation of the spirit of the Apocalypse.'[111]

*

A. T. Tolley has suggested that in some of the poems in Section II of *Poems 1937–42* Gascoyne 'was merely trying to reproduce the rhetoric of Jouve's poetry,' and that 'the violent, often conventional and decidedly unresonant diction was that of his model.'[112] The poet and critic Peter Levi rightly points to Gascoyne's 'ability to imbibe the essence of another poet and produce it as one's own: he has been through this mysterious process with Eluard, Jouve, Eliot, Wallace Stevens [...].'[113] Philip Gardner has observed with some acuity that the language Gascoyne uses in his translations of Jouve 'has sometimes a marked resemblance to his own densely packed lines in *Poems 1937–42*.' Certainly Gascoyne's mastery of the alexandrine – a difficult line-length to manage in English – derives from his knowledge of French poetry.'[114] This accords with Yves Bonnefoy's view, expressed in his essay 'Translating Poetry', that while 'the translator need [not] be ... a "poet" [. . .]' there is the implication 'that if he himself is a writer he will be unable to keep his translating separate from his own work.'[115] Tolley writes: 'Indeed, it is the over-ripe, archaic diction of *Poems 1937–42* that Gascoyne uses in translating Jouve.' His argument is that 'Jouve's *Kyrie* may have triggered for Gascoyne the conception of a body of visionary poems with a traditional religious centre. Certainly, poems from *Kyrie*, translated without the filter of Gascoyne's sensibility, could well be mistaken for pieces from *Poems 1937–42*.'[116] Tolley quotes a version by Keith Bosley of one of Jouve's poems in the section 'Les Quatre Cavaliers',[117] but it does not provide a viable illustration of the point he is making since there is no immediate or close association with Gascoyne's own diction. However, his reasoning is valid, and I would suggest that a line like the following from *Sueur de sang*, 'Space stricken with human sickness beneath the sky' (in Gascoyne's translation),[118] could serve as a more apposite example. It would hardly be surprising if Gascoyne's response to Jouve and to the poems he was translating at the end of the 1930s, had directly influenced his own work as he struggled to develop and refine a new poetic language. Gascoyne himself makes that point:

> The use of lines quoted from Jouve as epigraphs to certain sections of *Poems 1937–42* is insufficient indication of the enormous influence that his poetry, outlook, and conversation were to have on me for many years to come. Anyone familiar with Jouve's *Sueur de sang*, *Matière Céleste* or *Kyrie* will recognize this influence in such poems of mine as 'World Without End', 'The Fortress', and 'Insurrection'. [119]

He told Lucien Jenkins in the *Stand* interview that 'The poems after *Miserere* are all strongly influenced by Jouve. Even the poem which was originally titled "To Benjamin Fondane" and which is now "I. M. Benjamin Fondane"' [op. cit., p. 22]. There are, too, several examples of poems whose titles chime with those of Jouve's own.[120] When I showed Gascoyne the unpublished poem, 'Post Mortem', which I had transcribed from a notebook in the British Library, he immediately acknowledged Jouve's influence, but grimaced when he re-read, some fifty-five years on, the attempt to bring out the link between eroticism, the unconscious and death.[121]

Section V of *Poems 1937–42* begins with two lines from Jouve: 'Au temps ou la douceur / Est cruelle et le désespoir est brillant' / 'At a time when gentleness / Is cruel and despair is resplendent' (my translation); but the most significant appropriation occurs in the epigraph to Section I, *Miserere*:

> Le désespoir a des ailes
> L'amour a pour aile nacré
> Le désespoir
> Les sociétés peuvent changer

'Despair has wings / Love has despair / For shimmering wing / Societies can change', in Gascoyne's translation. Another of Gascoyne's 'ghost' collections of the 1930s was entitled *Despair Has Wings*,[122] also subsumed into *Poems 1937–42*. Almost seventy years on I have chosen his title for this volume of homage to both writers. Gascoyne broadcast a selection of his own poetry in 1949, and referred in his introduction to 'the octet' of poems, *Miserere*, with which the programme began:

> The title [...] is intended to indicate that the poems relate to a period of spiritual death and anticipation of rebirth – of spiritual rebirth and not of religious revival – and not only to such a period in the life of an individual, but to the present moment in the history of Western civilization, as is indicated also by the four brief lines from the French poet, Pierre Jean Jouve, chosen as an epigraph to the sequence [and quoted in French, as above].[123]

With reference to these four lines which underscore Gascoyne's profound empathy with Jouve's poetry, Brian Merrikin-Hill has pointed to 'the need to escape from the world into the territory of the spirit and the freedom (even dangerous freedom) in which the spirit belongs.'[124] He argues earlier in his penetrating essay that 'Gascoyne had learned from Berdyaev that freedom was the natural milieu or environment of the human spirit', and that from Chestov and Berdyaev 'comes also the realization that in this freedom one faces the black holes in oneself, one's own devil, the Jungian "shadow".'[125] An observation by Benjamin Fondane in his letter to Gascoyne of July 1937 (see endnote 59) is also pertinent to the chosen title for this celebration of Gascoyne and Jouve.

Fondane comments: 'There is something positive in despair, and you have recognized it.'[126] In the penultimate paragraph, he qualifies despair as 'an extreme way of thinking, radical, positive, with the possibility of liberation.'[127]

Three of Jouve's lines form the epigraph to Gascoyne's *Requiem*, written between 1938 and 1940, dedicated and presented to the South African composer Priaulx Rainier[128] in Paris just before the war:

> Permets que nous te goûtions d'abord le jour de la mort
> Qui est un grand jour de calme d'épousés,
> Le monde heureux, les fils réconciliés.[129]

Other lines from poems by Jouve are quoted in the *Collected Journals*:

> Le coeur divin en haut
> Tout devenant immense et irradié
> En haut plus près du bas
> Seulement si l'on est à l'intérieur et si l'on joue
> Tout pour le tout[130]

from *Matière céleste* in the entry for 12 February 1938; 'Nous avons etonné par nos grandes souffrances / L'inclinaison des astres indifférents' from *Kyrie*: 'Les Quatre Cavaliers', 23 January 1939, as mentioned above; and under the entry for 4 March 1940 Gascoyne inserts, also from *Kyrie*:

> Sans contact aujourd'hui je suis, sinon
> Avec le sein de Dieu
> Sans amour aujourd'hui je suis, sinon
> Dans les vallées de Dieu
> Et le soleil emprisonné par les forêts
> Le coeur, emprisonné par le ciel de la guerre.[131]

T. S. Eliot had intended to publish four of Gascoyne's Jouve translations facing the French originals in *The Criterion*, just before the war, but in the event he sent on the manuscript to Anthony Dickins at the *Poetry* (London) office, together with some of Gascoyne's own poems. Dickins mistakenly supposed (not unreasonably, as I have indicated) that the latter were also translations from Jouve. Gascoyne's letters to Dickins, 31 March 1939, and to Tambimuttu, 8 May 1939,[132] corrected the misunderstanding: 'The poems "De Profundis" and "Lachrymae" are <u>not</u> translations,' he pointed out. In the event, the first of his Jouve translations in *Poetry* (London) did not appear until Number 5, two years later.

In a manuscript notebook dating from 1941 (though some entries are as late as 1944) one of the pages is headed '<u>Pierre Jean Jouve</u>: <u>The Resurrection of the Dead</u>', with the titles of ten poems Gascoyne has translated or intends to translate: 'Insula Monti Majoris', 'Nada', 'Brow', 'Woman and Earth', 'Gravida', 'March 28th', 'Helen's Land', 'The Mother', 'Interior Landscape', 'The Two Witnesses', 'Kyrie'.[133] On an earlier page in the notebook, dated 20 February 1942, Gascoyne has listed '<u>Poems 1938[sic]–42</u>' under the heading '<u>New Project for a Collection</u>' where 'The Five Poems After Jouve' are: 'Woman & Earth', 'The Moths', 'Brow', 'Nada', 'Insula Monti Majoris'. However, in *Poems 1937–42* (1943) the last named poem is replaced by 'The Two Witnesses'.

*

Certainly, Gascoyne's passionate commitment to search for truth in his poetry chimes with that in prose of the existentialist philosophers Kierkegaard, Nietzsche and Sartre who were preoccupied by the possibility of authenticity. What Gascoyne particularly admired in Pierre Jean Jouve is clarified in an incomplete, unpublished draft in a notebook from *c*. 1950 in which he stresses his concern for the authenticity of being, allied to the notion of poetry as 'newly realized truth':

> Even among the poems that Jouve would now prefer to be forgotten, anterior to the first volume of his Poetic works, the long *Prayer* of 1923, written when this poet was thirty-five, remains still remarkable and valuable because of the blunt unhesitating force of robust sincerity that fills each line. It will always keep the freshness of a genuine immediate utterance of newly realized truth.[134]

Gascoyne emerges through this series of 'Metaphysical' poems in *Poems 1937–42* as a cartographer of man's spiritual crisis, his primary concern, while engaging at the same time with the severe crisis provoked by the ineluctable fact that the world was at war. On the very day that W. H. Auden was sitting in the Fifty-Second Street 'dive' composing his poem

'September 1, 1939', Gascoyne had articulated his despair in apocalyptic terms: '[…] but to witness the irredeemably tragic spectacle of mankind rushing blindly and incoherently, like the Gadarene swine, into a sea of horror and obliteration.' His poem 'Lowland' with its plain and valley depicts the lowest point or nadir that mankind has reached. The speaker's invocation: 'out of our lowland rear / A lofty, savage and enduring monument!' echoes the violence that is stressed in the metaphorical geological fission in 'Mountains': 'Pure peaks thrust upward out of mines of energy / To scar the sky […]. Schismatic shock and rupture of earth's core', give way to the apocalyptic: 'Preach to us with great avalanches, tell / How new worlds surge from chaos to the light'. His concern, however, extended to the future, too, and 'the coming spiritual revolution'.[135]

Consciously or unconsciously, Gascoyne's Surrealist imagery reappears in *Poems 1937–42*. The reader is aware of the ubiquity of the *eye* (sometimes disembodied) which witnesses all. This constant in the iconography of Surrealist writing and art is presented as 'both visual and poetic, as a site of confrontation, conjunction and communication. The eye,' Fiona Bradley explains, 'links inner and outer.'[136] In Gascoyne's 'Metaphysical' poems, the eye is 'hovering', 'a socket-free lone visionary eye';[137] 'searchlight eyes'. However, there are other equally relevant ways of interpreting the unmistakable presence of the eye(s). In his journal there is a reference to the 'absence of images' because 'the essential nature of the experience [is] negation',[138] Gascoyne comments that 'practically the only image that presents itself at all strongly is *a black vacuum in (or through) which two eyes are fixedly staring*' 22 August 1939.[139] Just as significant is a passage in Jouve's 'The Unconscious, Spirituality, Catastrophe' that foregrounds the notion of the all-seeing penetrating eye:

> Incalculable is the extension of our sense of the tragic that is brought us by meta-psychology, and even more incalculable [is] the extension of the knowledge gained by that eye which gazes into our secret parts – which eye is none other than our own.[140]

Gascoyne's principal concern is with that inner searching eye. C. A.

Hackett is in no doubt that 'With the examples of Baudelaire and Rimbaud before him (his debt to both is great), and equipped with the technique of Freudian psychology, Jouve has come to consider himself as fulfilling a prophetic function, as "l'oeil de la catastrophe", an eye which reveals and explores the tragic atrophy of both man and his civilization.'[141] Gascoyne had also written in his journal on 22 August: 'For the world a week of severe crisis has begun. For me, the interior crisis continues, more intense than ever. [...] Am I to become a sort of *Prophet* [my emphasis] after these days in the Wilderness?' On 31 August he had added, 'Having accepted the idea of myself as a kind of "prophet", I find the weight of this rôle increasingly overwhelming.'[142]

*

Tambimuttu wrote twice to Gascoyne in June 1945. In his letter of 8 June he sympathizes with the recipient: 'I understand how you must feel after this period of nerve strain and attrition and I do see that we must arrange for you to have a rest.' Tambi writes in the second letter, three days later, that he has arranged a two months' holiday in the Scilly Isles for Gascoyne, all expenses paid. 'I hope,' he continues, 'during that time you will be able to complete some of the books that we have commissioned from you – *for example, Pierre Jean Jouve translations*' [my emphasis].[143]

Tambimuttu wrote again to Gascoyne on 6 July 1945:

Dear David,
Will you let me have your translation of the Jouve poem during the next week? We want to publish this anthology as soon as possible, and I would greatly appreciate it if you will do this for me.
Yours,
T.[144]

The following year, Jouve inscribed to Tambi a presentation copy of *La Vierge de Paris*.[145]

Derek Stanford noted in December 1946: 'Meanwhile the poet [Gascoyne] is said to be preparing a volume of translations from Pierre Jean Jouve.'[146] But this did not materialize, although the intention was still there as drafts of translations and an incomplete preface to Jouve indicate in several notebooks dated *c*. 1950. In January 1946 Jouve's poem 'L'Espérance' (from *Hymne*, 1947) appeared in the original French in *Horizon*, No. 73; later in the year Jouve published his collection *La Vierge de Paris* (1939–44) which was inspired by a medieval statuette of the Virgin and child which 'he had kept in a recess in his study adjacent to his wife's consulting-room' in their rue de Tournon apartment.[147] The statuette figures in Gascoyne's poem, 'The Fabulous Glass' in Section IV of *Poems 1937–42*, dedicated to 'Mme B.R.-J.' (Dr Blanche Reverchon-Jouve):

> In my deep Mirror's blindest heart
> A Cone I planted there to sprout.
> Sprang up a Tree tall as a cloud
> And each branch bore a loud-voiced load
> Of Birds as bright as their own song;
> But when a distant death-knell rang
> My Tree fell down, and where it lay
> A Centipede disgustingly
> Swarmed its quick length across the ground!
> Thick shadows fell inside my mind;
> Until an Alcove rose to view
> In which, obscure at first, there now
> Appeared a Virgin and her Child;
> But it was horrid to behold
> How she consumed that Infant's Face
> With her voracious Mouth. Her Dress
> Was Black and blotted all out. Then
> A phosphorescent Triple Chain
> Of Pearls against the darkness hung
> Like a Temptation; but ere long
> They vanished, leaving in their place
> A Peacock, which lit up the glass
> By opening his Fan of Eyes;
> And thus closed down my Self-regarding Gaze.[148]

Five poems by Jouve from *Les Quatre Cavaliers* were published in the original French in 1946 in *Adam International Review*, No. 156–157.[149] In 1947[150] Jouve himself came to London (Allied Circle, 14 May) and Oxford (The

Taylorian Institute, 12 May) to give a lecture, *Apologie du Poète*,[151] and Gascoyne returned to Paris for the first time since 1939, staying for a year. During that period he submitted to Tambimuttu an essay that would be published in *Poetry* (London) as 'New French Poetry: A Paris Letter'.[152] 'Among the new collections of poems published during 1947,' he wrote:

> the most important is probably *Hymne*, the latest volume of the *Oeuvres Poétiques* of Pierre Jean Jouve (I can only say 'probably' in order to avoid seeming too uncategorically dogmatic on the subject) [...] (p. 32).

In the manuscript notebook, 'Poetry and Transcendence'[153] dated 1947, Gascoyne drafted anthologies under the headings 'The Return of the God-Conscious' and 'Poésie et Metaphysique Existentielle'. Authors represented included Jouve together with Apollinaire, Von Hofmannsthal, Tagore, Wahl, Cavalcanti, Claudel, Otto Rank, Valéry, Hölderlin, and Heidegger. The passages copied out for his Jouve entry are taken from the first section of *Apologie du Poète* (1947).[154] Later in the same notebook, another heading reads: 'Pages Copiées. A Common-place Book Miscellany', comprising extracts selected from works by Valéry, Rank, Pierre Jean Jouve, Michel Carrouges, Henri Thomas, Jankélévitch, Nicolas Berdyaev, Georges Bataille, Ramón J. Sender, René Char. For Jouve's contribution, Gascoyne has taken four paragraphs from the end of the last section of the lecture[155] and has also transcribed the poem 'Rôle du poète' from the collection *Hymne* (1947) on five pages.[156]

Gascoyne often visited Jouve who now lived in a studio near the Porte d'Orléans at 7 rue Antoine-Chantin, and first met the poet Yves de Bayser there. Margaret Callander has commented on Jouve's 'sustained preoccupation with all aspects of Baudelaire's life and work',[157] and she has emphasized his 'intimate and lifelong relationship' with the nineteenth-century poet.[158] Jouve's appreciation of Baudelaire in various publications during the war and after revived and increased Gascoyne's own interest.[159] In his contribution to *L'Autre* in 1982, Gascoyne comments: 'During the war I had had serious psychological problems[160] and when I resumed analysis [for a few sessions] with Blanche, I told her about the interior voices that attacked me, haunted me constantly and repeated, "The gods…the gods…the gods…the gods". But she couldn't do anything for me.'[161] It wasn't until 1960 that the voices finally left him, as he told Jeremy Reed.[162] Even in February 1995 he could say to his interviewer, Dennis Egan, 'Everything about me is a "case history".'[163]

*

If Gascoyne never completed that projected 'biographical and critical essay (5,000 words)', he did leave the fragments of a preface in two notebooks now in the British Library. In the first, a draft entitled 'The Genius of Pierre Jean Jouve', Gascoyne describes him as

> probably by far the most impeccable and fastidious of all living writers. He has never written an insensitive or carelessly expressed or superfluous paragraph in his life; in his way he is a perfectionist,[164] yet he would no doubt deny that he had ever achieved perfection, as all perfectionists will. […] His aim has always been to focus and communicate the *essential*'.

Gascoyne goes on to highlight in the *Oeuvres Poétiques*

> the rare quality of density. […] He is one of the most cultured and sober minds in Europe'. Balthus told journalist Françoise Jaunin that 'His [Jouve's] poetry was as pure as his personality was complex and difficult'.[165]

During the German Occupation a poetry of Resistance had emerged in France, 'a turning-point in the development of modern French poetry.'[166] In the much longer fragment, 'Jouve, Preface', Gascoyne focuses on *La Vierge de Paris*. 'The magnificent opening poem, "La Chute du ciel,"[167] is a prophetic apostrophe written immediately before the outbreak of war:

> Mais tu n'as pas perdu. Les anges de la guerre
> Les exterminateurs! ont mesuré ta face
> Mourante et animale auprès du flanc des tours
> Dans les rues balayées par l'eventail de pierre…

and surely nothing was written then or has been since that summed up the essential significance and inmost development of the historic events of the period that it announced. Further on,' he continues, 'the book contains, among several other long poems and sequences of interlinked short pieces, three series of poetic meditations which represent perhaps the greatest mystical poetry that Jouve has written; and this poetry will, I believe, be seen to take its place among the greatest and most authentic religious poetry in French literature.'

Looking back in the immediate post-war years on the period 1939–45 reflected in Jouve's *La Vierge de Paris*, Gascoyne is disturbed by the common currency of particular words and their general debasement:

> While throughout the whole of Christendom, and no less throughout Nazi Germany and Soviet Russia, discourses, exhortations and patriotic 'religious' utterances without number were using the words *sacrifice*, *renunciation*, and similar terms and expressions, the whole time that the war lasted, there were in Europe, here and there, a very few [...] men using the same words without at the same time blaspheming against the spirit without which language becomes in the end the instrument of a curse which man brings on himself.

> *Sacrifice* and *renunciation* refer to an inner experience entailing an essential movement and change of attitude in the very soul of the individual, and it is the lesson of what it is really to experience this movement that is mediated and grasped and given articulate expression in these poems.

Gascoyne is speaking specifically here about 'Nuits des Saints I & II' and 'Innominata', and concerned to underscore the great significance which 'must be attributed to the task the poet fulfils when he uses language as the French language has been here used by Pierre Jean Jouve.' That is to say, with its 'vigorous purity' when 'properly employed.'[168]

Another attempt to articulate his approving post-war response to Jouve's *La Vierge de Paris* is also incomplete, and again examines the nature of genius in relation to its subject:

> Pierre Jean Jouve: uncompromising, uncompromised witness to the eternal values, purest representative in our time of the most profound French genius. We speak of geniuses, but the most individual and solitary geniuses are paradoxically the agents of a single and identical genius, that of the national literature of their country. In modern France, who does not recognize this voice in Péguy, in Bernanos, in the passionate sobriety of Gide, in the patriarchal majesty of Claudel, – in

Pierre Jean Jouve, a man who stands apart from all political parties, all religious dominations, all literary schools, and has thus been able to speak of patriotism, of God, of cultural values with an authority which only those blinded by partisan prejudices can fail to recognize.

'Songe', 'Récitatif', 'La Chute du Ciel', 'Terres Promises', 'A Une Soie', 'Ode Funèbre': these six poems are surely among the greatest expression of the spirit of French religious patriotism and at the same time of the lonely man's longing for God and His Kingdom, in all the French poetry of this century. These are more truly poems of prophecy than anything to be found in the ...' [*Essay ends here*][169]

There is a stylistic difference in the work of each poet after the war; it is clear that both were disillusioned. Callander describes Jouve's response after the defeat of Germany 'to the spectacle of a divided, suspicious, hesitant Europe in which France failed to set an example of decisive, united action. He made no public expressions of reproach and bitterness,' she writes, 'but there are a number of small indications of anxiety and disappointment in his work at this time.' She argues that *Génie*, his first collection after *La Vierge de Paris*, is 'puzzling. It is very short, and yet the reader finds a great difficulty in picking out the main themes and the important images.'[170] Writing in 1988, Gascoyne recalled his increasing disappointment with 'post-war governments' failure to implement the dreams and promises of a radically improved new future that had helped the Allies bring the Third Reich to an end.'[171] In his case, he had had to accept his inability to write with the same facility. *A Vagrant and other poems* (John Lehmann, 1950)[172] represents a further stage in a developing vision. There is a readiness to experiment and a loosening of emotional tension in his acknowledgement of human frailty. The title poem is dedicated to marginality and solitude; the authenticity of what we read here is never in doubt.

Gascoyne contributed three unpublished translations of poems by Jouve to John Lehmann's BBC Third Programme series, *New Soundings* 12, broadcast on 11 March 1953: 'Young Spirit', 'Landscape in Another Direction' and 'Interior Landscape'.[173]

*

There is no record of the (in)frequency of correspondence between the two writers before or after the 1950s. However, two brief letters from Jouve to Gascoyne have survived, dated '14 décembre 1956', and '5 février 1957'.[174] In the first, Jouve had previously sent for comment a copy of his translation of *Macbeth*.[175] Gascoyne kept a letter and a note from Blanche: the first is dated '7 août' [no year], the second is undated but certainly written post-war as the first line only of the location of the Paris apartment indicates: '7 rue A[ntoine-] Chantin'. Without other evidence, it can only be tempting to speculate that the year was 1947 and that Gascoyne's impending visit to the Jouves would have been his first since 1939. It is interesting that while the writer addresses him as 'Mon cher ami', and 'Mon ami' respectively, she signs the letter quite formally as his analyst, 'B. R. Jouve', rather than 'Blanche'.[176]

During that decade Gascoyne, together with other poets such as Yves Bonnefoy and Yves de Bayser shared an intense admiration for Jouve, but they were concerned that he wasn't well enough known. Gascoyne ends his contribution to the *L'Autre* volume as follows: 'It seems to me that he rejected the glory which at the same time he desired.' In 1951, while he was in America with Kathleen Raine and W. S. Graham, Gascoyne made a recording for the Library of Congress in Washington of translations of six poems by Jouve.[177] His essay, 'A New Poem by Pierre Jean Jouve: "Language"', which includes two translations (the first of which has remained uncollected until now), was published in the *London Magazine* in 1955.[178]

In 1964, as he described in the Lucien Jenkins interview, Gascoyne suffered a serious breakdown[179] in Paris, where he had been staying with Meraud ['Mérode'][180] Guevara, the widowed painter. He had tried to get into the Elysée Palace, feeling he had a mission to see de Gaulle to warn him of a plot.[181] He was arrested in the Elysée Yard, forcibly taken to the *gendarmerie* and kept there for a whole afternoon. The police commissioner, M. [Jean] Rousselot, a poet himself according to Yves de Bayser, telephoned the British Consulate, then saw Jouve's name in Gascoyne's *carnet*. Blanche arrived, as did the Consulate representative who Gascoyne slapped in the face. Gascoyne was treated very gently[182] and taken to the *préfecture* psychiatric hospital in a straitjacket. She was one of the few people to visit him there, and 'This was in fact the last time I saw her,' wrote Gascoyne. 'She had been intermittently my analyst since 1938. I should perhaps rather say "counsellor", as she never undertook to "cure" me, and I never paid her a sou.'[183] Meraud Guevara had provided Gascoyne with accommodation at her homes in Paris and Aix-en-Provence for the previous ten years. Blanche Jouve advised her that 'it was very important that he should be released into the care of his mother and that he should not live alone.'[184] In his unpublished diary, 'My First Post-Apocalyptic Notebook', which he kept religiously during this enforced stay in the Vaucluse mental hospital on the outskirts of Paris, there is an entry for 'April 16th or 17th?' which reads: 'Blanche R.-J. is for me one of the true 20th Century Scientific (Freudian) Sybils. And a Sybil is an incarnation of the Divine Total(ly) Human (or Collective) Unconscious.'[185]

*

Gascoyne told Michèle Duclos in his interview with her that 'At times when one can't write poems oneself, [translation] represents a way of creating equivalents of poems that one likes or admires. Rarely have I translated a poem that I haven't liked.'[186] (In the essay 'Translating Poetry', Yves Bonnefoy makes the observation, 'If a work does not compel us, it is untranslatable.') Gascoyne continued, 'Above all, I like to translate poems by poets whom I know personally, because it seems easier to put myself into their frame of mind with that background knowledge.'[187]

Gascoyne's contribution to the First Cambridge Poetry Festival in 1975 was a reading of 'The Two Witnesses' by Jouve,[188] and after Jouve's death in 1976,[189] he would return to his work on many occasions, producing translations, articles and reviews. He translated four 'Mozart' poems in 1980 for *Adam International Review* No. 222/24 at the request of the editor, Miron Grindea, and contributed the short piece, 'My Indebtedness to Jouve', with its particular and apposite reference to music.[190] A handwritten list of items for a 'Possible Collection of Prose

Writings, criticism', dated 26 February 1983 in a red and black notebook, includes 'La rue de Tournon (to be written)'; it may have been the basis for Gascoyne's contribution, 'A Paris en 1937', to the special Jouve number of L'Autre (1982). The magazine Spectrum 3 published Gascoyne's translation of Bernard Groethuysen's preface to Jouve and Klossowski's Poèmes de la folie de Hölderlin in 1983. When Jouve's Folie et génie was published posthumously that same year, Gascoyne told the poet Jeremy Reed just how much he admired and valued the final text, 'Hölderlin', in the collection of radio broadcasts transmitted in 1951.[191] Two of Gascoyne's previous Jouve versions were included in The Random House Book of Twentieth Century French Poetry, edited by Paul Auster in 1982[192] and Gascoyne contributed in Spring 1984 to a series of radio programmes by O. Germain Thomas commemorating Jouve, broadcast by France-Culture.[193] In 1988, 'The Unconscious, Spirituality, Catastrophe' was reprinted as a pamphlet by Words Press, forty-seven years after its first appearance in Tambimuttu's Poetry (London).

The Times Literary Supplement issue of 6 May 1988 included Gascoyne's important review essay, 'The ascetic sensualist', on Jouve's Oeuvre, Volumes I, II. It was an opportunity, many years later than he had intended, to produce what is a penetrating, empathic and closely argued assessment and analysis of both poet and novelist. But while Gascoyne approached this task with some trepidation, as his letter to Alan Jenkins the commissioning editor makes clear,[194] he found himself reassured that the piece at the proofs stage was 'as it now stands exactly the article I intended to write.'

In 1996 Delos Press reprinted his translation of 'The Present Greatness of Mozart'. Selected Verse Translations, which appeared that same year, included twenty-two versions of Jouve, superseding the twelve in the Collected Verse Translations of 1970. Gascoyne was presented in London by the French Minister of Culture with the prestigious award of Chevalier dans l'Ordre National des Arts et Lettres in recognition of his services to literature and art in France. Sean Street visited him at his Isle of Wight home to talk about the art of translating verse; an edited recording was broadcast in the BBC Radio 4 Kaleidoscope feature, The

Cartographer of Thought, in September 1996.[195] When asked how he saw the role of the poet as translator, Gascoyne replied:

> Well, to make a poem which sounds like an English poem, but at the same time not to betray the image or the meaning too much. 'Beauty is truth, truth beauty' most people would agree with Keats, but truth is not the same as accuracy. There are translators who simply take the translation as a stepping stone to write a poem of their own. I try to make a poem that sounds good and corresponds to some extent to the original musical rhythm. French music is totally different.

As for Jouve's 'voice', he commented that 'he is a difficult poet to appreciate, I think, especially for English readers, because it's a very individual combination of sex and mysticism [...],' and through his knowledge of Freud, he was 'very much aware of the connection between sex and spirituality.' He added, 'Modern French poetry – a great many [French] poets are concerned with the question of *being*, which is something that English poetry readers find rather forbidding or pretentious [...]. I think maybe there's a reaction now.' During the course of the programme, Gascoyne read two Jouve translations, 'Woman and Earth' and the brief 'Spittle on the asphalt', observing that Jouve 'makes a very strange connection between spittle and spirituality.'

*

Asked in 1998 to evaluate the impact of Jouve on Gascoyne's life and work, Yves de Bayser, a friend of both men since the Liberation, replied: 'Elle était capitale' / 'It was of cardinal importance.' He continues:

> But if you want to talk about Pierre's influence *on* David's poetry, it seems to me that it can only be considered from a thematic point of view, as a development towards a holy spiritualism, since David's Christ is 'of Revolutution and of Poetry', and retains a great autonomy. He quotes Jouve in the epigraph to *Miserère*, but on the theme of spiritual suffering. One thinks, too, of the poem dedicated to Blanche Reverchon-Jouve ['The Fabulous Glass'] which is the expression of a poeticized sacreligious dream, but he is closer to the truth than Jouve when he talks of the influence of psychoanalysis on his [Jouve's] work. In Jouve's case it is obvious.[196]

Gascoyne commented to Duclos that Jouve 'was admirable and very difficult but always very kind to me, very encouraging,'[197] but it is the last paragraph of his letter to Jenkins that represents, in effect, his final word on the man who had meant so much to him:

> I have known quite a few poets/writers in my time, some of them well-known, but None have inspired in me the respect and admiration I felt before long for Jouve and his utter devotion to his craft and calling, his passion for the impeccable, his disdain for the inauthentic; at the same time his generosity and openness. So it is a considerable satisfaction to me to have got this article off my chest at last![198]

In a letter dated 15 February 1940, Balthus addresses his friend Jouve as 'a voice that is the last refuge of light in this dark night, a glimmer of the dawn to come.' How appropriate this is as an expression, too, of the very essence and promise of David Gascoyne's work.

Dr Roger Scott
Northumbria University

1 'Introductory Notes' to *Collected Poems 1988* (Oxford University Press, 1988), p. xvii.

2 'L'imagination vorace de David Gascoyne' (16 February), my translation. 'Gascoyne a ses maîtres. Au zénith: Rimbaud et Hölderlin. A un degré moindre: Pierre Jean Jouve. Il a un gourou: Jacob Boehme. Il a trouvé des guides, fort inconfortables il est vrai: Kierkegaard, Chestov, Fondane, Berdiaev'.

3 Skoob Books Publishing Ltd., 1991, pp. 283, 399. Elsewhere, Gascoyne notes the influence of Martin Buber.

4 'L'Etrange Mister Gascoyne' in *Libération* samedi et dimanche (22 January, 1984). My translation. He told Margaret Callander, author of *The Poetry of Pierre Jean Jouve* (Manchester University Press, 1965), that 'Journal entries seem determined by imponderable contingencies': letter dated 22 April 1989, p. 3. I am very grateful to her for photocopies of this and a later letter dated 6.VI.89, and for permission to quote from them.

5 *Poèmes de la folie de Hölderlin*, Pierre Jean Jouve, avec la collaboration de Pierre Klossowski. Avant-propos de Bernard Groethuysen (Paris: J. O. Fourcade, 1930). Groethuysen's preface, 'Concerning the Poems of Hölderlin's Madness', was translated by Gascoyne in *Spectrum* 3 (1983). See SECTION 2.

6 As he had no German, Gascoyne's own versions of the poems were made with the help of two German friends who were living in Paris at the time. See 'A Paris, en 1937...' in *L'Autre*, Jouve number (June, 1982), p. 11.

7 'Introductory Notes', p. xvii.

8 'Le Surréalisme et la Jeune Poésie Anglaise: souvenirs de l'avant-guerre' in *Encrages* (Université de Paris VIII–Vincennes, Summer, 1981), p. 16. He discusses 'the attraction which Jouve's poetry exerted over me, and its determining influence subsequently on my development', p. 17. My translation here. Samuel Beckett before him had been drawn to Jouve's work during the late 1920s. James Knowlson records that Beckett later confessed to a 'passion' for Jouve's earliest poems written before the First World War, prior to Jouve's conversion to Catholicism [and the rejection of all twenty of his pre-1924 published texts, as he explained in his postcript to *Noces* (1928)], and had read 'at least two' of the novels, *Le monde désert* and *Paulina*. See *Damned to Fame. The Life of Samuel Beckett* (London: Bloomsbury Publishing, 1996), p. 75. While he was at the Ecole Normale in Paris, Beckett had met Jouve but, according to John Pilling, 'had not

found him sympathetic': *Beckett before Godot* (Cambridge University Press, 1997), p. 27. Pilling states in an earlier study that 'although Jouve was "deeply haunted" by "the Nada theme, the theme of absence", Beckett's interest in him lapsed with his religious verse': *Samuel Beckett* (London: Routledge & Kegan Paul, 1976), p. 4. After taking his finals at Trinity College, Dublin in 1927, Beckett chose to focus his research essay on Jouve, Romains and 'Unanimisme' and assured Knowlson that he had completed the project in the summer of 1928. The paper has not surfaced.

9 *L'Autre*, p. 11. My translation here and subsequently. *La Symphonie à Dieu* (Paris: Gallimard, 1930) included one etching by Sima, who provided eighteen for *Le Paradis perdu* (Paris: Guy Lévis-Mano, 1938). Balthus provided a drawing for *Matière céleste* (1936), and a limited edition of Jouve's poem, 'Urne', with a frontispiece by Balthus, was published that same year by Guy Lévis-Mano. Jouve's poem, 'Un Tableau de Balthus', was included in *Génie* (Paris: Guy Lévis-Mano, 1948). Twenty-eight of the fifty-three copies of the limited edition of *Langue* (Paris: Editions de l'Arche, 1952) have three lithographs, by Sima, Balthus and André Masson. A watercolour by the latter illustrated the first edition of *Sueur de sang* (1933). The story 'La Victime' in *La Scène capitale* is dedicated 'A Balthus' in the first edition of 1935 and in that of 1948 only. Four contributions by Jouve from the 1940s relating to Balthus: 'A Balthus' [poème], 'Mémoire de Larchant' (poème), 'Oeuvre Peinte de Balthus', and 'Balthus', were collected in the exhibition catalogue *Balthus*, préface de Dominique Bozo (Paris: Musée National d'Art Moderne, Centre Georges Pompidou, 1983). In Gascoyne's last notebook, dated '1983–1995', he has made a fair copy of Jouve's poem, 'Balthus'; it was his practice to write out his own English version below or on the facing page. In this case, he never began the translation.

10 'What seduced me here,' wrote Jouve in *En Miroir*, 'was the painting as such: it was so exact, and precise, so intense in its embodiment of the carnal, that I considered *Alice* as my companion.' Quoted and translated by Robert Kopp in his essay 'Balthus and Pierre Jean Jouve. Previously Unpublished Documents', in *Balthus*, catalogue edited by Jean Clair (London: Thames & Hudson, 2002), p. 66

11 This may be a reference to *La Montagne / L'Eté* (1937), or to a later work, *Paysage de Champrovent* (1940). Jouve also bought Balthus's *Portrait de Thérèse* (1936) in 1937 and hung it over his desk. He kept both *Alice* and the *Portrait* for the rest of his life. Jouve's text, *Les beaux jours* (1945–6), was inspired by two of Balthus's paintings: *Paysage de Champrovent* (1942–5) and *Les beaux jours* (1945–6). See Jouve, *Oeuvre*, tome II, *Proses*: 'La Voix, le

Sexe et la Mort', p. 1206. Jouve's prose-poem, 'Le Tableau' (*Oeuvre*, tome II, pp. 1223–25) describes Balthus's *Alice* and the poet's fascination with her 'intense sensuality'. At one point, he is appalled to see an empty frame: Alice has vanished. See Richard Stammelman's perceptive analysis in his study, *Lost Beyond Telling: Representations of Death and Absence in Modern French Poetry* (Ithaca / London: Cornell University Press, 1990), pp. 108–9.

12   They first met in Florence in April 1921; she was a psychiatrist then. In 1928 Blanche was admitted to the Société Psychanalytique de Paris, three years after she and Jouve married.

13   He met Jean Wahl, Gabriel Marcel, Pierre Leyris, Pierre Emmanuel, Salah Stétié, and the painter, Balthus (brother of Pierre Klossowski, co-translator with Jouve of the Hölderlin poems). 'This was a wonderful privilege for me,' he wrote in the letter dated 22 April 1989 to Margaret Callander. Gascoyne also met the Irishman Desmond Ryan, one of his best friends till he died: 'Ryan became very devoted to Blanche and Pierre and helped them drive from Paris after the Fall of France in 1940.' Letter, op. cit., p. 2. According to Daniel Leuwers's 'Repères chronologiques' in *Europe, revue littéraire mensuelle*, No. 907–908 dedicated to Pierre Jean Jouve (November–December 2004), Jouve and his wife left Paris on 11 June 1939, stayed from July to November in Dieulefit, then moved to Cannes in 1941, eventually arriving in Switzerland that same year. From the Autumn they lived in Geneva at 2 rue du Cloître, close to the Saint-Pierre cathedral, and did not return to Paris until September 1945. Op. cit., p. 129. Ryan, too, was one of Blanche's patients. After failing his medical for military service, Gascoyne worked briefly as a ship's cook on the Solent, taking over from Ryan.

14   Mentioned by Virginie Monnier in her essay, 'Before the War (1932–39)', in the *Balthus* exhibition catalogue edited by Jean Clair, p. 236. See Elisabeth Roudinesco, *Histoire de la psychanalyse en France*, 2 volumes (Paris: Editions du Seuil, 1986), pp. 110–15.

15   Tome XL (March, 1933), pp. 353–85, signed jointly. The text is reprinted in *Pierre Jean Jouve: Oeuvre* tome II (Paris: Mercure de France, 1987), pp. 1556–91, and introduced as follows: 'Ce texte [...] constitue un repère dans l'histoire de la psychanalyse en France' (p. 1555).

16   *The Poetry of Pierre Jean Jouve*, p. 125.

17   According to Gascoyne, 'Blanche was a most unorthodox Freudian in the way she encouraged her patients to mix socially.' Letter to Callander, 22 April 1989, p. 2. The poet Yves de Bayser, a regular guest at the post-war Thursday evening sessions, was taken aback when he first got to know the Jouves to learn that Blanche, a Freudian psychoanalyst, was a practis-

ing Catholic and received Communion. She told him 'calmly and firmly: "Freud n'est pas parole d'Evangile / Freud is not gospel".' De Bayser 'loved, admired, revered Blanche'. I am grateful to Dr Alan Munton for permission to quote from a letter sent him by de Bayser, dated 3 March 1998. In 1984, Gascoyne recalled a conversation with Mme Jouve many years previously when he had commented to her: 'It seems to me, Blanche, that your method of analysis is closer to Jung's than to Freud's'; and her reply: 'Well, that's interesting, but I've never found time to read him.' My translation. See Michèle Duclos, 'Entretien avec David Gascoyne', *Cahiers sur la poésie* No. 2, Numéro special David Gascoyne (Université de Bordeaux III, 1984), p. 12.

18   Published in two volumes, *Hécate* (1928) and *Vagadu* (1931). It is interesting to note that, reviewing *Collected Poems* (1965) in the *London Magazine* (November 1965), the poet Gavin Ewart claims that Gascoyne 'uses verse (as most poets do) like a kind of *private psychoanalysis*' [my emphasis]: 'A Voice from the Darkness', p. 91. Philip Toynbee did not share Gascoyne's admiration for Jouve's achievement in *Aventure de Catherine Crachat*: his article in *The Times Literary Supplement*, 'The Prose of Pierre Jean Jouve', 24 April 1948, found 'the Catherine Crachat series, *Hécate* and *Vagadu*, [...] among the most *baffled* novels of our time. They are the work of a Samson Agonistes blindly struggling with a medium which seems to become more intractable with every page.' And further, 'the idea itself is powerless to be born' (p. 225). However, for Toynbee, Jouve 'gloriously justified his previous labours in prose' with *La Scène capitale*. His earlier novels become at once intelligible' (p. 225). The front cover of the *Europe* number devoted to Jouve poses beneath his portrait the intriguing question, 'Psychanalyste et écrivain?' / 'Psychoanalyst and Writer?', reversing the expected word order; however, this is the title of another section in the review, and there is no connection with Jouve. The response of Anaïs Nin, who first met Gascoyne in 1936, is of interest here. She never forgot that he had brought her some books by Jouve and with them 'a new world, new dreams, a new poison, a new drug. The first to treat the knowledge of psychoanalysis as a poet, to write a novel which is half a poem.' See *The Journals of Anaïs Nin*, Vol. II 1934–1939 (London: Peter Owen, 1967), p. 272. Earlier in her diary she notes: 'Pierre Jean Jouve has described a world in which visions, hallucinations, symbolism, usually relegated to our night life, operate in full daylight, and in union with the body fusing desire and fantasy, dream and action, reverie and passion. He does not pretend to illumine everything. He does not construct all the bridges, chronology, sequences, to which we usually cling, because they

are not a part of life. In life we have these sudden illuminations, sudden blanks, sudden shadows, sudden abysses.' Ibid., p. 127.

19 Letter to Callander, 6 June 1989, p. 2.

20 'Blanche Jouve fut pour Jouve ce que fut Beatrice pour Dante [...]' in Jouve, *Oeuvre* II, p. 1727. This short piece was dictated as Wahl was blind and died a few weeks later. Jouve's prose poem, 'Trésor', in the section *Proses* in *Oeuvre* Tome II (1987), p. 1262 is addressed to Blanche: 'J'ai un trésor qui est toi [...]'.

21 *Twentieth-Century French Literature*, translated by Louise Guiney (Chicago/London: University of Chicago Press 1983), p. 210.

22 Editor, *Anthology of Second World War French Poetry* (Glasgow: University of Glasgow French & German Publications, 1994, 1999), pp. 117–18. Toynbee wrote in 1954: 'M. Jouve is a Freudian [...] and on one level Freudian terms can unravel nearly all the mysteries of his philosophy. Thus to have accepted the discoveries of Freud and to have transmuted them for his high creative purpose is by no means the least of his achievements. Many have attempted this transmutation, but perhaps only James Joyce has won an equivalent victory over the intractable material. M. Jouve is also a Christian, though inquisitors would find a rich crop of heresies in his books.' 'The Prose of Pierre Jean Jouve', op. cit., p. 227.

23 *The Cambridge Introduction to French Poetry* (Cambridge University Press, 2003), p. 147.

24 Op. cit., p. 148. In the introduction to his edited volume, *20th Century French Poems*, Stephen Romer refers to 'Pierre Jean Jouve, whose more systematic study of Freud and of sexuality resulted in some inimitable symbol-laden poetry' (London: Faber & Faber, 2002), p. xxiv.

25 Gascoyne's review, 'The ascetic sensualist', of Jouve's *Oeuvre*: Tome I, Tome II, in the *Times Literary Supplement* (6–12 May 1988), p. 505. Reprinted in *Selected Prose 1934–1996*, ed. Roger Scott (London: Enitharmon Press, 1998), pp. 343–48. See **Appendix A1**.

26 Gascoyne told Mel Gooding, who interviewed him at his home in 1991, that he 'taught himself to play "Mikrokosmos", studies for piano.' See 'Interview summary' of Tape 4, side 4, F1383, National Sound Archive: NLSC 'Artists' Lives': Gascoyne, David, 1916–2001, p. 3.

27 Letter to Callander, 22 April 1989, pp. 3–4.

28 It is important to acknowledge, too, the significance of Jouve's art criticism or 'poésie critique', as that work by twentieth-century French poets has been called. Jouve wrote essays on Courbet, Delacroix and Meryon, as well as Balthus, and four of his poems represent a direct response to Claude Lorrain's paintings. See Marcel Raymond, 'Pierre Jean Jouve

devant les peintres' in *Pierre Jean Jouve*, (eds.) Robert Kopp et Dominique de Roux (Paris: *L'Herne*, 1972), pp. 345–51, and Robert W. Greene, 'Spiritual Quest and Scriptural Inquiry: Pierre Jean Jouve's Art Criticism', in *Conjunctions: Verbal-Visual Relations* (Essays in honor of Renée Riese Hubert), edited by Laurie Edson (San Diego State University Press, 1996), pp. 211–27. Gascoyne told Duclos that 'the essay on Courbet, in his [Jouve's] *Tombeau de Baudelaire*, is a masterpiece.' Op. cit., p. 23. Margaret Callander expresses with acuity 'the rich and multi-layered resonances in Jouve's work of other artistic Modes,' referencing his 'intense and reflective response to certain musicians, painters, the "phares" of his creative life.' Jouve's affinities can be seen as 'eclectic', as she says: Mozart, Berg, Delacroix, Balthus, Meryon, Giacometti – all of these 'linked to his visions of disaster and reconciliation.' See her article in *French Studies*, LXVI, No. 2 (April, 1992), p. 227.

29 Vol. 1, No. 2 (February), pp. 84–94. This translation was included in *Mozart's Don Juan*, by Pierre Jean Jouve, translated by Eric Earnshaw Smith (London: Vincent Stuart, 1957), pp. 1–10. Published separately in 1996 by Peter Baldwin's Delos Press. See **SECTION 2**.

30 'My Indebtedness to Jouve', in *Adam International Review*, 422/24 (1980), pp. 52–3. Included in *Selected Prose 1934–1996*, p. 125. See **Appendix A2**.

31 First published in *Seven*, No. 5 (Summer 1937), p. 33. See **Appendix A3** for drafts of this poem. Gascoyne's translations of four poems by Jouve relating to Mozart were published in *Adam International Review*, op. cit.: 'Tempo di Mozart', 'Mozart dans la fosse commune', 'Viaticum', 'Don Juan', pp. 48–9. I found the draft of another, fifth version, from *Matière céleste*, 'O joie de tant d'années. Et toi flute enchantée' in the notebook dated '1983–1995'. No pag. See **SECTION 1**.

32 'A Toi, quand j'écoutais ton arc-en-ciel d'été'. For Jouve, 'The only human parallel to this rarified emotion [the particular joy of spiritual illumination] is [...] the music of Mozart.' Callander, pp. 86-7.

33 Letter to Callander, 22 April 1989, p. 4.

34 See **Appendix A4** for 'First Draft' and 'Second Draft'. The first draft is in the Manuscript Department at the British Library, Adds. 56041, 56043, the second in the Berg Collection in New York Public Library. In a ledger-sized notebook *c.* 1950, Gascoyne listed 'Works by Alban Berg: (bracketed) Wozzeck – Buchner; Lulu – Wedekind ; / Piano Sonata; / (bracketed) String Quartet, Lyric Suite / Clarinet pieces; / (bracketed) Concerto for Violin, Piano & Chamber Orchestra, Violin Concerto; / (bracketed) Four songs (with orchestra), Four Postcard-text Songs (with orchestra), Der Wein (aria with orchestra); / Three Pieces for Orchestra. Op. 6'. No pag.

35　It was first published in *Cahiers du Sud*, No. 220 (Marseilles) in January 1940, pp. 49–52, then in *Poems 1937–42*, Section III, Editions: Poetry, London (Nicholson and Watson, 1943), pp. 25–9, and reprinted in *Collected Verse Translations*, edited by Alan Clodd & Robin Skelton (Oxford University Press, 1970), pp. 115–121. See **Appendix A5**.

36　He agreed that there might have been something in my suggestion that there was, too, the feeling that nothing would ever be the same again after Berg's death and in view of the deterioration in international relations in Europe. What does seem incontrovertible is the elegiac mood; however, instead of maintaining the initial focus on Berg and his music and their significance for the poet, the 'Strophes élégiaques' open out in section two to engage with the *zeitgeist* defined by the palpable threat of imminent war, and the notion of mankind hellbent on a collision course with catastrophe.

37　Quoted in my essay in the e journal, *Temporel* numéro 2, October 2006 [http://temporel.fr], edited by Anne Mounic: 'Gascoyne Translating / Translating Gascoyne. Gascoyne traducteur / Traduire Gascoyne', which introduces the first series of self-translations of his own poems by Gascoyne, which I discovered in various notebooks after his death. The second part of the translations is due to appear in *Temporel* numéro 3 in May 2007. The texts of the poems appear in both English and French.

38　See Section II, 'Musique et poésie ou "Les Moyens réciproques du mystère"', in *Fascinations musicales. Musique, Littérature et Philosophie*, edited by Camille Dumoulié (Paris: Editions Desjonquères, 2006), p. 129. I am very grateful to Jean-Yves Masson for sending me a copy of his paper first given in 2003.

39　'Alban Berg 1936'.

40　Published in a limited edition in 1952, and by Mercure de France, 1954: 'Dédié à l'esprit d'Alban Berg'.

41　*Wozzeck ou le nouvel opéra*. 'It is in Alban Berg that Jouve discovered the musician to whose technique he felt most attuned,' writes Callander. 'He was always impressed by the reconciliatory quality of Berg's music.' Op. cit., p. 281. Jouve and Fanu collaborated on what Gascoyne calls 'two books of musically technical and poetic analysis of Alban Berg's operas *Wozzeck* and *Lulu*.' See *Adam International Review*, op. cit. There is a series of four poems entitled 'Lulu' I–IV in Jouve's collection *Moires* (1962), where he writes in 'Phrase IV: 'La plus grande vertu s'attache à la musique / A l'imprévu des lignes de sons et des constructions / Harmoniques pareilles aux fosses marines / Idées enjouées tragiques d'invention.' See *Oeuvre* I, p. 1117.

42   'Jouve on Berg': 'The Concerto has two parts, which are divided into several lesser interlinked sections. It begins (Andante – Introduction) with a most strange undulating movement, a series of fifths based on the four notes of the *cordes vides* of the violin, which in becoming re-engendered in multiple fashion in every register of the orchestra, and so acquiring an impressive density, expresses most wonderfully a predestined grace, nervously alert and opening upwards to the shower of heaven's favours as to a gradual efflorescence of Danaean gold.' No pag. Incomplete, unpublished.

43   Beinecke Collection, Yale University. The next page contains a list of poems from '*Les Noces* (Vol. 1. of *Oeuvres Poétiques*)' under the title 'P. J. Jouve', the titles listed are: 'Noces'; Songe'; 'Enfants Mystérieux'; 'Des Déserts'; 'Sancta Teresa'; 'Humilis'; 'Sept Fleurs'; 'Jardin des Ames au Printemps'; 'La Symphonie à Dieu'; 'Incarnation'; 'Le Père de la terre'; 'Vrai Corps'. No pag.

44   See interview with Michel Remy in *Temenos* 7, ed. Kathleen Raine (London, 1986), p. 270.

45   Interview with Lucien Jenkins in *Stand*, Vol. 33, No. 2, double issue (Spring 1992), p. 21. Reprinted in *Selected Prose 1934–1996*, pp. 47–53.

46   'The ascetic sensualist', op. cit.

47   Quoted and translated by Robert Kopp in his essay 'Balthus and Pierre Jean Jouve', op. cit., p. 64. Graham Dunstan Martin, editor and translator of the *Anthology of Contemporary French Literature* (Edinburgh University Press, 1972), writes that 'though he [Jouve] claims to obtain his images from the unconscious, he regards his poems as organisms, each having its own inbuilt system, exercises very tough intellectual control over them, and often uses a fairly strict form,' p. 2.

48   Op. cit., p. 22.

49   This note represents his response to the publication of Jouve's *Langue* (1954): 'Those who today are able to recognize in Jouve the most important poet at present writing in France, may well be proud that he is this is objectively to be deduced from a just appreciation of the veritable content of his writings. I am thinking now of *Langue* […].' No pag.

50   *Stand* interview, op. cit., p. 22. Nevertheless, in his essay in *Encrages*, Gascoyne makes the fascinating claim that 'Jouve, in my opinion, remains one of the greatest of all the Surrealist poets,' p. 17. In the poetry anthology, *Le Surréalisme et ses alentours*, edited by Serge Baudiffier and Jean-Marc Bebenedetti (Paris: Classiques Larousse, 1992), six poems by Jouve are included in the section 'Les alentours du surréalisme': five from *Les Noces* and one from *Sueur de sang*, pp. 156–62. In his masterly study *The*

Truth of Poetry, Michael Hamburger affirms that 'Surrealist practice retained its hold on French poets up to the fifties and sixties.' He places Jouve together with Eluard, Reverdy, Michaux and Char. (London: Anvil Press, 1996), p. 194. David Gervais's essay, 'On French and English Poets', refers unequivocally to '*Surrealist* [my emphasis] poets like René Char, Pierre Jean Jouve and the poets who follow in their wake', in *PN Review* 145 (May–June 2002), p. 32.

51   On 1 August 1977 Gascoyne responded by letter to a writer planning an article on British Surrealism. In the course of his reply (written by his wife, Judy, because of problems with a nerve in his right hand) Gascoyne explains: 'I gave up writing Surrealist poetry at the end of the thirties because I got sick of it, and then I came under the influence of Pierre Jean Jouve *who combined psycho-analytical imagery with Christian mysticism*. [My emphasis]. I don't think I could ever have been described as "generally Christian Platonist"[…].' I am very grateful to Marcus Williamson who emailed me a copy of the letter. Both Elizabeth Jennings and Terence Tiller see Gascoyne as a mystical poet. Jennings believes that his work 'leads directly back to the visionary poetry of Vaughan, Herbert and Traherne,' and argues that 'it is emphatically of this time and this place – concrete, rooted, exact.' She contends that 'even where Gascoyne is, on the one hand, most objective or, on the other, most involved and personal, the mystical, visionary element is always present: if not in the lines, then between them.' See 'The Restoration of Symbols: a study of the poetry of David Gascoyne' in her *Every Changing Shape* (London: Longmans, 1961), p. 194. Tiller's observation in this regard is that the key to Gascoyne, 'if one word may be taken as a key, is surely mysticism? – the personal quest for immediate knowledge and experience, to be obtained by spiritual exercise on what he calls "the sunless but how dazzling plains" of symbolic thought.' Tiller points to 'the agonies and splendours and excitements' of this quest. From a photocopy of the typescript of 'David Gascoyne', written by Tiller, produced by Patric Dickinson, broadcast on Monday, 9 December 1946, 8.20–8.40 p.m., p. 1. Again, I'm grateful to Dr Alan Munton.

52   *Encrages*, op. cit., p. 17. In July 1938 Jouve contributed to *La Nouvelle Revue Française* an article entitled 'La Musique et l'Etat Mystique / Music and the Mystical State'.

53   'The ascetic sensualist', op. cit. My translation here of Jouve's statement.

54   Ibid.

55   Philip Gardner, 'David Gascoyne' in Donald Stanford (ed.), *Dictionary of Literary Biography*, Vol. 20: *British Poets, 1914–1945* (Detroit, Michigan: Gale Research Co., 1983), p. 144.

56 He would write, 'Each man must undertake alone and in silence the task of creating a new spiritual reality with which to fill the Void [...],' in 'Note on Symbolism: its role in metaphysical thought', *Poetry Quarterly*, Vol. 8, No. 2 (Summer 1946), pp. 77–8. Reprinted in *Selected Prose 1934–1996*.

57 See Starobinski's preface to Jouve's *Les Noces suivi de Sueur de sang*, Collection Poésie (Paris: Editions Gallimard, 1981), p. 18. My translation.

58 'Introduction' to his translations, *Friedrich Hölderlin: Selected Poems* (Bloodaxe Books, 1990), p. 9.

59 And Benjamin Fondane, too, after an exchange of letters. Gascoyne told Ramona Fotiade that Jouve and Fondane 'were among the first poets to recognize the crucial importance of Baudelaire as the creator of modern poetry.' Interviewed 15 August 1994. See *Bulletin de la Société d'Etudes Benjamin Fondane*, BSEBF, No. 3 (Spring 1995), p. 7. My translation. Gascoyne wrote to Fondane on 24 July 1937. Fondane's reply, dated 'Juillet 1937' and long thought to be irretrievably lost until I found Gascoyne's handwritten copy of it in one of the poet's notebooks in the British Library Manuscript Collection, is printed in BSEBF for the first time, with a prefatory note by Fotiade, pp. 2–4.

60 The publication includes an Introduction, pp. 1–14. He adds: 'The poems which follow are not a translation of selected poems of Hölderlin, but a free adaptation, introduced and linked together by entirely original poems. The whole constitutes what may perhaps be regarded as a *persona*,' p. 14. Gascoyne acknowledges below the 'helpful criticism' of his two German friends, Marianne Donhauser and Carl Wilhelm Böhne. Since 1938 versions of a further eight poems by Hölderlin have been published, two of which are not to be found in *Poèmes de la folie de Hölderlin*; they are included in Gascoyne's *Selected Verse Translations*, edited by Alan Clodd & Robin Skelton, with an introduction by Roger Scott (London: Enitharmon Press, 1996), pp. 77–83.

61 No. 11 (July 1938), p. 76

62 'Books of this Quarter', Vol. XVIII, No. 70 (October 1938), p. 406.

63 'David Gascoyne' in *The Freedom of Poetry* (London: Falcon Press Ltd., 1947), p. 46.

64 Philip Gardner, op. cit., p. 144.

65 Germaine Brée discusses the incorporation into *Sueur de sang* of 'a large variety of myths and mythic figures: the descent into death and the re-ascent toward life suggest the myth of Orpheus.' Op. cit., p. 210.

66 *David Gascoyne ou l'urgence de l'inexprimé* (Nancy: Presses Universitaires de Nancy, 1984), p. 26. My translation.

67 *Collected Journals 1936–1942*, p. 192.

68 *L'Autre*, p. 12. My translation.
69 *Collected Journals*, p. 197.
70 *L'Autre*, p. 12.
71 *Collected Journals*, p. 198.
72 Ibid., p. 202.
73 Ibid., *L'Autre*, p. 12. My translation. I have found the statement 'La mariée est trop belle' problematic. Initially, I thought there might be a Freudian explanation, given the later journal entry for 10 November 1938: '[…] I have a masochistic attitude towards my father, whom I imagine to be punishing me all the time!' according to Blanche (op. cit., p. 213). But then I felt that Blanche's use of the expression must relate to David's failure to develop and to take to fruition so many of his ideas for poems, stories, essays, books. I'm very grateful to both Michael Hamburger and Yves Bonnefoy who were kind enough to provide their own responses to my query, and who tend to confirm the latter suggestion. Hamburger wrote (letter dated 17 September 2004) that 'My interpretation of Blanche Reverchon's words is not Freudian. What it implies, for me, is that the exaltations got in the way of the hard work needed for their realization in writing. They were too beautiful in themselves. Of course that may have been connected with an analysis of David's sexual problems […]. But in David's case, which I experienced at first hand when he stayed with us in London, [it] had to do with a failure to apply himself to the hard work. Hence the resort to drugs – another substitute for the application.' Bonnefoy (email sent 19 September 2004) is not sure about the full implications of the expression 'La mariée est trop belle'. Are we to understand that the beauty of the wife paralyzes the husband? he asks. 'That would correspond closely to the feeling of impotence David experienced [when] confronted by his own projects, these ideas that came to him.' According to Bonnefoy, what characterized Blanche's approach to her patients was her enigmatic manner of expressing an elliptical judgement while looking you straight in the eye with an air of understanding, as if it were obvious that you comprehended what she was saying though it was not explained. As for her psychiatric practice, 'it was undoubtedly a case of suggestions, of priming, to oblige the analysand to reflect.' I have tried to give as accurately as possible the gist of Bonnefoy's illuminating response in French.
74 *Collected Journals*, p. 202.
75 Ibid., p. 205.
76 'Isn't it pride that's preventing you from speaking?'
77 Ibid., p. 239. However, he observed in the previously mentioned inter-

view with Patrick Mauries that 'analysis had been interrupted by the war':
Libération, 22 January 1984.

78 *The Sun at Midnight* (Enitharmon Press, 1970), 33 (no pag.).

79 (Paris: Gallimard). In his own copy of Charles Madge's collection *The Disappearing Castle* (London: Faber & Faber 1937), Gascoyne has marked three lines in the section 'Fragments 1933–36', p. 88: 'The white clouds rise and rise behind the lifted knife / The sky barbarians, the unlife / Rise behind the trees' raised arms, rise and rise.' He has added to them a quotation from Jouve's poem, 'Ta ruine, église de Larchant' in *Kyrie*, the last three of nine lines, as follows: 'L'écho est le cri d'angoisse sous mon coeur; / Le ciel écoute les barbares: bruissement / Lointain de fer et plaies en movement.' I am very grateful to Matthew Waterhouse who kindly sent me this information in November 2006.

80 Ibid., p. 243. *The Malahat Review*, No. 39 (July 1976) included this section (p. 16) as part of a longer extract in the year of Jouve's death, predating Alan Clodd's publication of *Paris Journal 1937–1939* in 1978 (London: Enitharmon Press).

81 *Collected Journals*, p. 257.

82 See **Appendix A6**. There are differences, too, in the two versions of 'Brow' first published in *New Directions*, No. 7, then in *Poems 1937–42*. However, 'Nada' was virtually identical in both its first publications: in the second stanza, 'All that which is' becomes 'All things that are'; 'And which is born' is changed to 'And yet are born'. 'The Moths' is identical in both *Poetry* (London), No. 5 (March–April, 1941) and *Poems 1937–42*. 'I continually wanted to improve the translations,' he told his interviewer Sean Street in 1996, speaking on the BBC Radio 4 Kaleidoscope feature, 'The Cartographer of Thought', in September 1996.

83 Gascoyne's translation was reprinted as a pamphlet by Words Press in 1988. See **SECTION 2**.

84 Dated 24 November 1940, 21 Grove Terrace, Teddington, Middlesex. He goes on to refer to pieces he has written on the American poets Kenneth Patchen and Hart Crane. The latter, sadly, seems to have been lost; it was never published.

85 Op. cit., pp. 89–90, 121–2.

86 Add. 56045 in the British Library Manuscripts Department. The collection, though very much in his mind for many years afterwards, was another project that never came to fruition. For example, in a notebook in the British Library dated 1950, Gascoyne lists 'Twelve Future Books' and the second, after 'The Sun At Midnight', is 'Introduction to Pierre Jean Jouve'. There is further evidence of Gascoyne's commitment to

Jouve and his work in a manuscript notebook, 1941, now in the Beinecke Rare Book and Manuscript Library, Yale University. I owe a debt of gratitude to Timothy Young, Kevin Repp, and Rebecca Findlay Lloyd for the considerable help I have received. Under 'Note 2 [for projects]' the tenth item in the list is 'Translation of Jouve's "Combat of Clorinda and Tancred" [sic]', no pag. *Le combat de Tancrède et Clorinde* was first published in the review *L'Usage de la Parole* (February 1940), then as a section of *La Vierge de Paris* (Fribourg 1944; Paris 1945). There is a note: 'N.B. Send Edwin Muir […] copies of individual poems, including five poems after Jouve ("Woman & Earth", "The Moths", "Nada", "Brow", "Insula Monti Majoris").' No pag. On another page Gascoyne has written the heading: 'Poems by Pierre Jean Jouve from "Porche à la Nuit" and "Vers majeurs"': *Porche à la Nuit* (Ides et Calendes, Neuchâtel, 1942); *Vers majeurs* (L.U.F. Fribourg, 1942). Both texts then appeared as separate sections of *La Vierge de Paris* (1944; 1945). Gascoyne has copied out the poem 'La respiration des arbres …' from *Porche* on the left hand page, leaving the opposite page blank for his English version. 'La fleur est le regard riant de la ruine' from *Vers majeurs* is also copied out in full, and he has translated the first line and part of the next on the right hand page: 'The flower is the ruin's smiling gaze / And this smile …' Later in the notebook, under the title 'Selected Poems 1933–43', the fourth item in the list reads: 'Selected Verse and Prose of Pierre Jean Jouve'. There are at least three attempts to draft a list of contents for a proposed book to be called 'The Naked Eye'. Each of the schemas includes 'texts in context', or 'miscellaneous extracts from a Commonplace Book'. Jouve is listed with many other writers. No pag.

87 Jouve's 'Vivre libre ou mourir' in prose was included in issue 29 of *Fontaine* in 1943; between 1940 and 1942 he had contributed several poems to five numbers of that review. However, it is just possible that Gascoyne might be referencing Rolland-Simon's article in the March issue, 1942: 'Spiritualité de Pierre Jean Jouve'.

88 Jouve's influence is palpable here. In Gascoyne's translation of 'The Unconscious, Spirituality, Catastrophe' the following line clearly indicates the source of his alternative heading for Section II: 'Incalculable is the extension of our sense of the tragic that is brought us by *metapsychology*' [my emphasis].

89 'Woman and Earth', 'The Moths', 'Brow', 'Nada', 'The Two Witnesses'.

90 Entry on 'David Gascoyne' in *Contemporary Poets* VII (London & Chicago: St James Press, 2001).

91 Jouve's poetry, he writes, 'posits a world of seemingly irreconcilable contraries, which the poet seeks to harmonize.' *Encyclopedia of Literature in*

the World, Vol. E-K (St James Press, 1999), p. 571.

92   *Oeuvre* I, p. 526.

93   *The Price of an Eye* (London: Longmans, 1961), p. 135.

94   'A Modern Inferno' (Saturday 5 February 1944), p. 68. Adam Piette reads the title of Gascoyne's poem 'Inferno' as 'a trope for the Blitz' which he sees 'as apocalypse'. *Imagination at War: British Fiction and Poetry 1939–45* (London: Macmillan Papermac, 1995), p. 46.

95   *Collected Journals 1936–1942*, p. 243. Gascoyne was always interested in the Apocalypse: he gave a talk on the subject at St James, Piccadilly on 14 June in the early 1980s [the actual year is not known]. The readings he chose included his translation of Jouve's preface, 'The Unconscious, Spirituality, Catastrophe', Jouve's poem 'The Resurrection of the Dead', and eight of his own from *Poems 1937–42*: 'Kyrie', 'Inferno', 'Mountains', 'Insurrection', 'The Open Tomb', 'The Three Stars', 'Epode', 'Zero'.

96   Op. cit., pp. 193, 194.

97   'Angry Waiting', a review of *Selected Poems* (London: Enitharmon Press, 1994) in the *Times Literary Supplement*, 15 December 1995, p. 21. It is relevant to point out that in his plan for a 'ghost' collection in the late 1930s, *The Conquest of Defeat*, subsumed into *Poems 1937–42*, Gascoyne included the title 'Apocalyptic Ode' in the proposed section 'Poetry on Contemporary and General Themes'. It was never written, or has not survived.

98   'The Unconscious, Spirituality, Catastrophe'.

99   Op. cit., pp. 193–4.

100 What is intriguing here is the impression that the English and French Surrealists' perception of the unconscious differed considerably. The art historian Dawn Ades points out that Gascoyne's fellow Surrealist poet, Hugh Sykes Davies, provided an unexpected take on Freud's notion of the unconscious in his lecture 'Biology and Surrealism' delivered at the International Surrealist Exhibition in London in 1936: 'While Breton saw the exploration of the unconscious as a liberation,' she writes, 'Sykes Davies saw it as a conquest; the unconscious was not a magic realm to be revealed, but a source of fear and hysteria.' See *Dada and Surrealism Reviewed*, exhibition catalogue (London: Arts Council of Great Britain, 1978), p. 348. Two years earlier, Gascoyne himself, reviewing a joint exhibition by Borès, Beaudin and Dalí at the Zwemmer Gallery had described an etching by the Spaniard as mediating '*the horrors* of the subconscious' [emphasis added]. See *New English Weekly*, 24 May 1934, p. 139. Quoted by Nigel Vaux Halliday in *More than a Bookshop: Zwemmer's and Art in the 20th Century* (Philip Wilson Publishers, 1991), p. 152.

101 Subsequently, Jouve would return to and elaborate particular points, as

in *En Miroir*. In his 'Commentaire à *Vagadu*' he stated that: 1. 'The unconscious exists at every moment, on a scale much vaster than the conscious mind, and humans have access to it through emotion; 2. Affective unconsciousness is dominated by sexual or erotic energy; the opposite pole, equally primitive, is the death instinct; 3. The growth of an unconscious sexual life, in every human being, is accompanied by guilt, or in other words by the sense of a profound transgression.' Quoted and translated by Robert W. Greene in his essay, op. cit., p. 214. Greene argues that in the preface to *Sueur de sang*, a 'pivotal text', Jouve's 'sure, supple deployment of terminology that must have been pristine at the time (e.g., *inconscient, libido, sur-moi, condensation*) is nothing short of dazzling. Obviously, Jouve had digested an utterly new vocabulary and mastered the conceptual system carried by the new lexicon. In the process he has assimilated basic Freudian notions and combined them with his deepest spiritual beliefs.' Ibid., p. 212.

102 Preface to *Les Noces suivi de Sueur de sang*, Collection Poésie (Paris: NRF Gallimard, 1981), pp. 18–19. My translation.

103 'The ascetic sensualist', op. cit. For Gascoyne, *Sueur de sang* 'together with its two pre-war sequels, is perhaps most representative and distinctive of Jouve's post-1925 output.' He adds, 'In all that he wrote, as in his character, asceticism is inseparable from sensuality. The mystical and the erotic constantly alternate or merge in his work.' Ibid. Michael Sheringham highlights the importance of Jouve's preface: 'the title [...] provides a key to his poetry and fiction, where the links between eroticism and spirituality, sexuality and death, the unconscious and the apocalyptic, poetry and the absolute, are paramount.' Entry on Jouve in *The New Oxford Companion to Literature in French*, edited by Peter France (Oxford: Clarendon Press, 1995), p. 417.

104 Quoted by Gascoyne in his *TLS* review, op. cit. (1988), and translated in his *Encrages* article, op. cit.: 'Spittle on the asphalt has always made me think / Of the face painted on the veil of holy women'.

105 'La catastrophe la pire de la civilisation est à cette heure possible parce qu'elle se tient dans l'homme, mystérieusement agissante, rationalisée, enfin d'autant plus menaçante que l'homme sait qu'elle répond à une pulsion de la mort déposée en lui. La psychonévrose du monde est parvenue à un degré avancé qui peut faire craindre l'acte du suicide. La société se ressouvient de ce qu'elle était au temps de saint Jean ou à l'an mille: elle attend, elle espère la fin.'

106 '[...] aujourd'hui les instruments de la Destruction nous encombrent; les iniquités pourrisantes des nations font de l'Europe "la grande prostituée

… assise sur une bête écarlate couverte de noms de blasphème ayant sept têtes et dix cornes ....'" Jouve's beast (in Revelation 17: 3–6) is the Whore of Babylon astride the Seven-Headed Dragon, as in Hans Burgkmair's woodcut *The Whore of Babylon*, or in Albrecht Dürer's *The Woman of the Apocalypse and the Seven-Headed Dragon* (Revelations 12: 1–6) of 1498. Both are in the British Museum collection.

107 Nevertheless, in stanza two of the 'Misterioso' section of *Strophes Elégiaques à la mémoire d'Alban Berg* Gascoyne writes: 'telle la fume / Qui accompagne la Bête hors de l'abîme, l'agneau / Meurtri, et ces chevaliers aux quatre couleurs criantes . . .' / 'Like the smoke that accompanies the Beast out of the Abyss, the wounded / lamb, and these horsemen of four glaring colours.' Here is apocalyptic imagery borne out of the fear created by the imminence of war, recalling the tone of Jouve's preface to *Sueur de sang*, linked with and directly referencing his 'Les Quatre Cavaliers' section in *Kyrie*.

108 Germaine Brée contends that in *Sueur de sang* Jouve reveals 'death and sexuality in league to obstruct the paths leading to redemption.' Op. cit., p. 210. For Gascoyne, however, the road to redemption is blocked by a wilful lack of belief on the part of mankind. Many years later, Gascoyne would write in his book of aphorisms, *The Sun at Midnight*: 9: 'Cosmic cruelty has caused the perversion of Nature, and above all human nature, on our planet. Man is not the cause but the vessel of wrath, the diseased victim and the intended instrument of this temporally disastrous working through process. But the cure of man's great illness has been long revealed and known. Now it is time to *understand* how what we call Redemption really works.' Op. cit.

109 'Les poèmes de cette anthologie ont été choisis [...] comme "témoins", c'est à dire, selon leur rapport avec l'événement catastrophique et à proprement parler apocalyptique de la Guerre.' My translation.

110 Quoted and translated by Robert Kopp, op. cit., p. 71, from Jouve's 'Avant-propos' to *La Colombe* (Edition de la Librairie de l'Université, Fribourg, 1943), pp. 16, 17. 'Le poète représente, dans la catastrophe et contre elle, ce qui est plus permanent et sacré que toute action politique. Seul le dépasse, en perfection de gravité, l'homme qui met sa vie dans la balance, et se bat. [...] Le véritable poète, celui des "choses essentielles", qui met en jeu les forces de l'âme et en fait un acte éternel, s'est toujours trouvé en face de l'événement par le même acte où il se trouvait en face de son temps. [...] Alors le poète [...] est seul [...] à pouvoir "posséder la vérité dans un âme et un corps"; il est seul chargé de ranimer les graves instincts d'amour, contre les séduisants instincts de mort.'

111 Op. cit., p. 199.

112 *The Poetry of the Forties* (Manchester University Press, 1985), pp. 143–4.
Keith Bosley, too, emphasizes that 'several of Gascoyne's own poems
[…] bear the unmistakable imprint of the master,' in a letter to the *Times
Literary Supplement*, 20–26 May 1988, in which he welcomed Gascoyne's
'generous review two weeks earlier of the Mercure *Oeuvre* of Pierre Jean
Jouve', p. 555. Bosley adds, 'Jouve's four extraordinary novels remain
unknown here: it is high time these early explorations of the Freudian
concept of Personality – especially the first, *Paulina 1880* (1925) – were
admitted to the Anglo-Saxon canon of "modern classics".' Ibid.

113 In his review of *Selected Poems* (Enitharmon Press 1994), in *Agenda*, Vol. 32,
Nos. 3–4 (Autumn–Winter, 1994–5), p. 288.

114 Entry on Gascoyne in *Dictionary of Literary Biography*, edited by Donald
Stanford, Vol. 20, *British Poets 1914–1945* (Detroit, Michigan: Gale Research
Co., 1983), p. 144.

115 *PN Review*, No. 45 (1985), p. 6, translated by John Alexander & Clive
Wilmer.

116 Frances Carey is an example of a critic under this misapprehension.
In her essay 'The Apocalyptic Imagination: between tradition and
modernity' in *The Apocalypse and the Shape of Things to Come*, ed. Carey
(British Museum Press, 1999), she mistakenly assumes that Gascoyne
himself 'who published work of an apocalyptic tenor' wrote 'The Two
Witnesses'; in fact she is quoting as an example one of the five Jouve
translations in *Poems 1937–42*.

117 'Nous avons étonné par nos grandes souffrances' / 'We have amazed by
our great suffering', from *Kyrie*, in *An Idiom of Night*. Poems by Pierre Jean
Jouve, selected and translated by Bosley (London: Rapp & Whiting, 1968),
p. 41. Gascoyne quoted the first two lines from this poem in the journal
entry for 23 January 1939, p. 243. Bosley's translation is as follows: 'We
have amazed by our great suffering / The inclination of the indifferent
stars / We have stared at the blood of the wound / With an outsider's
eye, in secret we / Have coupled through the false back door, / We have
become these iron systems / Which wander distanceless, caterpillar
horsemen / Of the last judgment, a vast, dismal boredom / Bears us to
your hoof of consummation / Red Horse black Horse yellow Horse white
Horse.'

118 See *Selected Verse Translations* (London: Enitharmon Press, 1996): 'From
Sueur de sang II', p. 96.

119 'Introductory Notes' to *Collected Poems 1988*, p. xvii. Margaret Callander
comments that 'the ever-recurring desire to affirm the miraculous nature

of resurrection leads Jouve into tortuous excesses of imagery, and the more sustained and rhetorical nature of this poetry gave licence to a habit of play on words that tends to weaken the mystery that it should illumine.' A footnote points to 'the same tendency in David Gascoyne, *Poems 1937–42*, Poetry London Editions 1943, especially in sections I and II, where Jouve's influence is most strongly marked.' *The Poetry of Pierre Jean Jouve*, op. cit., pp. 217–218.

120 Such as: 'Kyrie' / *Kyrie;* 'Sanctus' / 'Sanctus' (*Kyrie*); 'Mountains' / 'Montagnes' (*Matière céleste*); 'Tenebrae' / 'Ténèbres' (*Matière céleste*); 'Landscape' / 'Paysage mystique' (*Matière céleste*), 'Paysage intérieur' (*Kyrie*); 'Orpheus in the Underworld' / 'Orphée (*Matière céleste*); 'Inferno' / 'Enfers' (*Les Noces*); 'Mozart: sursum corda' / 'Mozart' (*Les Noces*); 'The Resurrection of the Dead' / 'Resurrection des morts' (*La Vierge de Paris*); 'The Fault' / 'La Faute' (*Le Paradis perdu*).

121 Add. 56045, p. 62b. See **Appendix A7**.

122 A journal entry by Gascoyne for 30 May 1938, reads: [between August 1937 and March 1938] 'I wrote *Hölderlin's Madness*, and *Despair Has Wings.*' On 10 August 1938: '– must revise *Despair Has Wings*, and make another effort to find a publisher for it': *Collected Journals 1936–1942*, pp. 171, 198.

123 'David Gascoyne: A Selection of His Poetry Made by the Author', first transmitted Sunday, 29 May and repeated Tuesday, 7 June 1949. I am very grateful to Erin O'Neill at the BBC Written Archives Centre, Caversham Park, Reading, who could not have been more helpful in providing me with vital information about Gascoyne's involvement in BBC broadcasts during the 1940s and 1950s, which was considerable.

124 'The Transparent Mirror', a review in *Temenos*, 7 (London: 1986) of M. Remy: *David Gascoyne ou l'urgence de l'inexprimé* (Presses Universitaires de Nancy, 1984), and A. Breton & P. Soupault: *The Magnetic Fields*, translated by David Gascoyne (London: Atlas Press, 1985), pp. 279–80.

125 Ibid., p. 275.

126 'Il y a du positif dans le désespoir, et vous l'avez vu.' My translation.

127 'Je le [le désespoir] tiens pour une pensée extrême, radicale, positive, pour une possibilité de libération.' My translation.

128 Jouve inscribed a copy of his study, *Le Don Juan de Mozart*, second edition (Paris: L.U.F., Egloff, 1944) to Rainier on the half-title: 'Pour Priaulx Rainier / ce témoignage pour ta Musique / avec grande estime et amitié. / Pierre Jean Jouve. / Paris 1946.'

129 'Grant that we may savour thee on the day of [our] death, which is a great day of wedded peace, the world happy, the sons [of men] reconciled.' My translation. The libretto was not set by Rainier until some years after-

wards. *Requiem* was first performed at the Victoria & Albert Museum on 15 April 1956, the occasion of its first publication in the programme. Chronologically, it belongs with *Poems 1937–42*, like 'Elsewhere', 'Concert of Angels', 'The Sacred Hearth' and 'The Plummet Heart'.

130 'The divine heart on high / All growing immense and radiant / On high closer to the depths / Only if one is within and if one gambles / Everything.' My translation here and below.

131 'Without contact today I am, otherwise / In God's breast / Without love today I am, otherwise / In God's valleys / And the sun imprisoned by the forests / The heart, imprisoned by war-torn skies.

132 See **Appendix A8**.

133 I have been unable to find any record of versions of 'March 28th' or 'The Mother'. This notebook is now in the Beinecke Rare Book and Manuscript Library, Yale University. No pag.

134 'The Philosophic Work in the Writings of Pierre Jean Jouve', in a notebook, *c.* 1950, in the British Library Manuscript collection. No pag.

135 *Collected Journals 1936–1942*, pp. 261, 253–54.

136 *Surrealism*. Movements in Modern Art (London: Tate Gallery Publishing, 1997), p. 70.

137 Roger Cardinal explains how 'In the wake of Rimbaud, it has been an article of faith for visionary poets that, in certain climactic moments or "illuminations", the eye sheds the encumbrances and distortions of conventional seeing': 'Approximating Giacometti: Notes on Jacques Dupin's "Textes pour une approche"', in *From Rodin to Giacometti. Sculpture and Literature in France 1880–1950*, eds. Keith Aspley, Elizabeth Cowling, Peter Sharratt (Amsterdam-Atlanta, GA: Editions Rodopi BV, 2000), p. 155.

138 *Collected Journals 1936–1942*, p. 256. Jouve himself acknowledges in *En Miroir*, 'his diary without dates', that 'The Nada [Nothing] theme [is] present in nearly all my work [...]. [It] has deeply haunted and pursued me.' See Bosley, *An Idiom of Night: Poems by Pierre Jean Jouve*, pp. 11, 14.

139 *Collected Journals 1936–1942*, p. 256.

140 'Incalculable accroissement du tragique que nous donne, la métapsychologie, et d'abord la connaissance d'un oeil qui est dirigé vers notre secret, de notre oeil même'. Eyes feature in three poems by Jouve in *Sueur de sang*: 'Oeil des cheveux', 'L'Oeil de la chevelure', and 'Combat des yeux' where the poet lays emphasis on 'l'oeil profond' and 'l'oeil déraciné'.

141 Editor, *Anthology of Modern French Poetry. From Baudelaire to the Present Day* (Oxford: Basil Blackwell, 1976), p. 288.

142 Op. cit., pp. 255, 259.

143 From a correspondence folder in the Gascoyne Collection in the Beinecke Rare Book and Manuscript Library, Yale University.

144 In the British Library Manuscript collection.

145 Without direct reference to Gascoyne's translation of 'The Unconscious, Spirituality, Catastrophe' in *Poetry* (London) Vol. 1, No. 4, or to his versions of two poems, 'Nada' and 'The Moths' in Vol. 1, No. 5 (both 1941), Jouve wrote: 'Pour Tambimuttu / qui publie mes ouvrages de ce temps en / langue anglais / avec une très amicale pensée / Pierre Jean Jouve. / Paris. Juin 1946'. This was the full edition of 305 pages (Paris: Egloff, Fribourg et L.U.F., 1946).

146 Presumably the volume first projected in 1940. 'David Gascoyne' in *The Freedom of Poetry. Studies in Contemporary Verse* (London: The Falcon Press, 1947), p. 69. Stanford has been one of the most perceptive of commentators on Gascoyne. The 'Note on contributors' in *Adam International Review*, No. 156–7 (March–April 1946) reads: '[David Gascoyne] At present is preparing a volume of translations of Pierre Jean Jouve's poems,' p. 23. The list of 'ghost' books, or 'Unfulfilled Promises' of Editions *Poetry* (London), as Alan Smith called them, contains three titles relating to works by Jouve: *Défense et Illustration, Le Don Juan de Mozart*, and *Poems*. The last appeared on the rear cover of *Poetry* (London) No. 12 (November–December 1947) as *Pierre Jean Jouve*, 'Selected Poems (trans.)'. See Alan Smith, '*Poetry* (London) 1939–1951', offprint from *Antiquarian Book Monthly Review* (April–May 1979), Section G, p. 15. It seems reasonable to assume that Gascoyne was the unnamed translator.

147 'Introductory Notes' to *Collected Poems 1988*, p. xviii. 'The child's face [was] obliterated by an iconoclast or time', but there is a sinister transformation of this description in Gascoyne's poem 'The Fabulous Glass'. The first, and much shorter, edition of *La Vierge de Paris* had come out in 1944 (L.U.F., Fribourg).

148 The poem incorporates a 'half-rhyming versification of a sequence of images that actually occurred to me during a psychoanalytic session with Mme Jouve in late 1938 [...].' Ibid., pp. xvii–xviii. It is interesting to note Gascoyne's use of upper case letters to give due weight to elements of each of the four visions passing across the mirror of his unconscious, and viewed by that constantly searching inner eye. He told Michèle Duclos that he noted down the images as soon as the session ended because 'they seemed to be charged with significance.' He added that the image of the peacock comes from alchemy, but he only realized it after the poem was written. Op. cit., p. 35.

149 pp. 4–6: 'Lorsque', 'Cheval Blanc', 'Cheval Roux', 'Cheval Noir', 'Cheval Jaune'. Gascoyne's poem 'Elsewhere' was included in the same issue, p. 9, its first printing.

150 Two of the Jouve translations, 'Woman and Earth' and 'The Two Witnesses', were included in *A Mirror for French Poetry*, edited by Cecily Mackworth (London: Routledge) that same year. Philip Toynbee was to raise Jouve's profile on this side of the Channel with his two articles in *The Times Literary Supplement*: 'The Prose of Pierre Jean Jouve', 24 April 1948, op. cit., pp. 225–27, and 'Self-Revelation of a Writer', 24 September 1954, p. 607. His searching, closely argued review in the first of these examines Jouve's *Aventure de Catherine Crachat* (Paris: Egloff, 1947) as I pointed out in an earlier citation, together with René Micha's study, *La scène capitale de Pierre Jean Jouve* (Brussels, 1942). In the second, Toynbee inspects Jouve's *En Miroir. Journal sans date* (Paris: Mercure de France, 1954), prefacing his commentary as follows: 'He is known best as a poet, and known, perhaps, to some of us for the beautiful translations of his verse made by his friend and admirer Mr David Gascoyne,' p. 607.

151 The French text was published by Guy Lévis-Mano in Paris in October, 1947. In his address Jouve spoke of 'Inconscient, Spiritualité et Catastrophe', his avant-propos to *Sueur de Sang*: 'It was less a "philosophy of writing" than a spiritual vision from some events, and based very precisely on the three words in the title' [my translation]: 'C'était moins une "philosophie de la composition" qu'une vision spirituelle à partir de certains faits, et reposant très exactement sur les trois termes du titre.' Reprinted in *Oeuvre* I, op. cit. Gascoyne discusses the substance of that lecture (first delivered in Brussels at the Séminaire des Arts, 18 December 1946) in *New Departures* 15, op. cit. Reprinted in *Selected Prose 1934–1996*. Jouve began his lecture 'saying that Elizabeth Barrett Browning's phrase referring to the poet as the sayer of essential things was one that had recurred to him throughout his life.' Gascoyne took him to see an exhibition of English poets' manuscripts which he found absorbing. See *L'Autre* article, p. 13. It is interesting to note that when Gascoyne's only play, *The Hole in the Fourth Wall* or *Talk, Talk, Talk*, produced by Elizabeth Sprigge, opened in London at the Watergate Theatre in the Strand from 1–7 March 1950, the poet and Sprigge read Gascoyne's translations of poems by Jouve and new poems of his own during the interval at each performance. In addition, in the author's note for the programme, Gascoyne quoted Elizabeth Barrett Browning to make his own point as a playwright: 'The poet should be [...] he who says what is essential; and in the theatre, he should try harder, if possible, than anywhere else, to express

the essential things [...].'

152 No. 13 (June–July, 1948), pp. 31–34.

153 It seems likely that 'transcendence' in the notebook's title indicates his concern with a spiritual rather than an aesthetic truth.

154 Paragraphs seven and nine, beginning respectively, 'Tous les grands poètes ont su que le conflit du fond et de la forme n'existait pas – [...]', and 'Si l'on pense que les formulas de "l'unité" variant avec les styles des époques [...]', op. cit., pp. 1184–85 in *Oeuvre* I (1987).

155 The extract begins: 'Pour la poésie, mystique est intimement liée à création [...].' The final sentence ends '[...]: de nos jours, comme au temps du romantisme, on peut laisser dans le combat sa raison,' op. cit., pp. 1202–04 in *Oeuvre* I.

156 pp. 657–658 in *Oeuvre* I.

157 *French Studies* 48, No. 2 (1994), p. 231. A review.

158 *French Studies* LXVI, No. 2 (April 1992), p. 227. A review.

159 *Tombeau de Baudelaire* (1942, 1958); editor of *Baudelaire, Choix de Textes: I Poésies* (1943), *II Critique* (1944), with prefaces; preface to *Les Petits Poèmes en Prose* in *Oeuvres complètes* (1955). See Interview with Mel Gooding, Tape 5, side B, F1384. Gascoyne bought a copy of the *Choix de Textes: I Poésies*, signing and dating the front free endpaper 'David Emery Gascoyne. London. March 1946.' He already owned *Charles Baudelaire* (Paris: GLM, 1939) which he signed 'David Emery Gascoyne. London. Summer 1943' and Baudelaire's *Le Spleen de Paris* (1937). In a journal entry for 16 August 1939 he wrote: 'Reread Baudelaire. Had never quite realized before, how much "in line" he is. He never covers up the fundamental worst. He records an intensely intimate experience of the metaphysical problems which are most important to me at the moment (tho' he does not fully exteriorize them, as I am trying to do).' See *Collected Journals 1936–1942*, op., cit. pp. 252–53. There is a page of reflection on Baudelaire's poem 'Le Voyage à Cythère' in Gascoyne's 'Poetry and Transcendence notebook, 1947'. On the final page he has made a list of titles by French writers including Sartre's *Baudelaire* and Benjamin Fondane's essay 'Baudelaire et l'expérience du gouffre'. No pag. In a 'Commonplace notebook, 1948' there is an entry, 'Notes for Baudelaire Play Project', with a synopsis outlining a dream and Baudelaire's relationship with Jeanne Duval who has left him, then been found and rescued from a brothel. A list of characters follows. In the same notebook, Gascoyne has copied out extracts from sections of essays by Baudelaire on Gautier, Wagner and Victor Hugo. Both notebooks are now in the Beinecke Rare Book and Manuscript Library, Yale University. No pag. So far as I know, Gascoyne never translated any of

Baudelaire's poems after his laborious adolescent attempts with a dictionary.

160 He 'took refuge' with Kathleen Raine during the 1940s and, as she described in volume 2 of her autobiographical trilogy, *The Land Unknown* (Hamish Hamilton, 1975), 'he used to say that it was as if his "brain leaked" (he later described it as "like a transistor set inside his head"), on which all kinds of voices not his own spoke, wept, declaimed, argued, chanted; while others would say, "we are the gods, the gods".' A visit to the Tavistock Clinic was unsuccessful: the Freudian psychiatrist who interviewed him said [anticipating Blanche's response], 'I'm afraid I can do nothing for you', op. cit., pp. 162–3.

161 He adds, 'I had a long conversation with [Jacques] Lacan about these phenomena', pp. 12–13. Gascoyne told Duclos that '[Blanche Reverchon Jouve] was a very distinguished psychiatrist who influenced Lacan a great deal – no-one has recognized this,' op. cit., p. 12. My translation. He made a similar comment to Mel Gooding, op. cit., Tape 3, side B, F1382, p. 3. There is a poignant unpublished poem addressed to these voices, 'Yes, You!' in a notebook dated c. 1950. See **Appendix A9**. In another notebook from 1950, the heading, 'Bile and spleen, nausea, self-reproach', precedes a further attempt to produce another poem in which he confronts the intolerable, tormenting voices, also in **Appendix A9**. At least there is a recognizable rhythm and a regular rhyme scheme, but some passages are disturbing to read, revealing a tenuous hold on reality; it is as if the need to write and the practice of jotting (in a large, wandering and spidery hand) are barely enough to stave off mental collapse. The fragment of a projected poem, 'Silence in Heaven', in a notebook in the Berg Collection in New York Public Library indicates Gascoyne's continued mental instability, abandoned with the words 'Poem sabotaged by demonic raving and impatience, 29.XII.52'. Another, longer fragment of what was intended to be a companion piece, 'Silence on Earth', begins: 'Always the voices […].' Gascoyne explained in his contribution to *Encrages* that he didn't find it strange that he 'could always distinguish the words "the gods, the gods",' because of what he knew of Hölderlin's experience. Op. cit., p. 23. My translation. Kathleen Raine questioned my failure, in the introductory essay I wrote for my edition of Gascoyne's *April: a novella* (London: Enitharmon, 2000), to 'give enough importance to the influence on David of Mme Jouve who gave him a long Freudian analysis […] David's novella makes really very good use of Freud's ideas, the repressed English girl and the Frenchman who does in fact choose her for that quality, as "Max" points out at the end.' In a letter sent to me

dated 29 October 2000. However, in a telephone call four days later during the evening of 2 November, she made it clear that she considered that 'Blanche's Freudian analysis of David did him irreparable harm.' Kathleen was always very protective of David.

162 Mentioned to me by Reed in a telephone conversation in April 2004.

163 See 'A Surrealist at the Elysée', in the *Independent on Sunday*, 12 February, Books section, p. 30.

164 Add. MS71704D. One aspect of this is the following, described by Gascoyne in *L'Autre*. On several occasions after their first meeting, Gascoyne received from Jouve texts which he had had printed as limited editions specially for his friends. For his manuscripts, he had to have only the finest paper and of the precise size he wanted. He would rule lines so that the dedication in his tiny narrow handwriting would run perfectly straight across the page. Op. cit. On this point, a French bookdealer's description of an inscription by Jouve reads amusingly as follows: 'extraordinaire calligraphie pattes de mouches'.

165 Quoted in Kopp, op. cit., p. 75.

166 Gascoyne, 'Departures' in *New Departures*, 15 (1983), edited by Michael Horovitz, p. 56.

167 From the sixth stanza of the poem, in the section entitled 'Gloire'.

168 Add. MS70714H (1944–1950).

169 There is no heading for this piece dating from 1948, but it clearly connects with the incomplete 'The Genius of Pierre Jean Jouve' from which I quoted previously. On an earlier page from this 'Commonplace book, 1948', Gascoyne has the same heading, 'The Genius of Pierre Jean Jouve' above 'Introductory Essay' (title only) followed by 'Selected Poems (translated): "Young Spirit"; "Summer"; "Frontier" [later "Boundary"]; "Pastoral of the Black Wind"; "Magie"; "Woman and Earth"; "In Helen's Land"; "A Woman Sleeps Alone" [published as "A Lone Woman Asleep"]; "Austere Nudity"; "I did not see that woman's back in vain" [published as "From *Sueur de sang*"]; "The sky is hidden" [published as "The sky is intimately hid"].' Sadly, Gascoyne's versions of 'Summer', 'Boundary', 'Magie' and 'Pastoral of the Black Wind' have not survived.

170 Op. cit., pp. 259–60, 261.

171 'Introductory Notes' to *Collected Poems 1988*, p. xix.

172 Two years earlier, Gascoyne's list, 'A Portfolio of New Poems, 1948' in a Commonplace notebook of the same date, included 'Poems from Hölderlin – Jouve – Supervielle'. In the event, translations of three poems by Supervielle appeared in the published volume. Beinecke Collection, Yale University, no. pag.

173 John Glen was the reader of the poems. The first of the three was cut from the recording but the script retains it. Again, I am indebted to Erin O'Neill at the BBC Written Archives Centre.

174 See **Appendix A10**. I am very grateful to Judy Gascoyne who located the originals and sent them to me.

175 The set of unbound proofs of *Shakespeare: Sonnets, version française par* Pierre Jean Jouve (Paris: Mercure de France, 1955) is still on Gascoyne's bookshelves.

176 The items are in Correspondence folder 29 in the Beinecke Collection. See **Appendix 11** for my transcription. I am grateful to Richard Lund of Northumbria University for his help in deciphering parts of both letters.

177 'Dear Lord pay no attention to my voice', 'Boundary', 'Young Spirit', 'Summer', 'The Sky is intimately hid', 'Evening Prayer', 'End of the World'.

178 Vol. 2, No. 2 (1955). It is included in *Selected Prose 1934–1996*. See **Appendix A12**.

179 He had seemed to recover from his first breakdown after the war, although according to his mother 'he had no proper treatment [because] he just would not co-operate.' See Dennis Egan, 'A Surrealist at the Elysée' in *The Independent on Sunday*, 12 February 1995, p. 30.

180 De Bayser's spelling, letter, op. cit., p. 8.

181 Gascoyne told Egan that the headline in the Paris newspaper, *Le Canard Enchaîné* read: 'He took himself for the Messiah'. Egan writes: 'Gascoyne admitted that his intention to inform de Gaulle that he was the Messiah sounded "spectacularly crazy", though he saw himself "fundamentally just as sane a person" as he ever was.' Op. cit.

182 Ibid., pp. 8–9.

183 Letter to Callander, 22 April 1989, p. 1.

184 Egan, op. cit. Gascoyne returned to the Isle of Wight accompanied by a male nurse.

185 From the collection of Gascoyne MSS and notebooks in the Library of the University of Tulsa. The poet, novelist and memoirist, Henry Bauchau (b. 1913), settled in Paris in 1946. Seriously depressed, he underwent psychoanalysis with Blanche Jouve from 1947–51. She helped him to discover his vocation as a writer and would become 'la Sybille' in his novel *La déchirure* (Paris: Gallimard, 1966), two years after Gascoyne had written his diary in the Vaucluse mental hospital and used the name 'Sybil' in reference to her.

186 Op. cit., p. 30. My translation. Cf. Robert Lowell who said of his *Imitations* (1958) that he had produced them 'when I was unable to do anything of my own'. Quoted by Carmine Di Biase in his review of *Mario Praz: Bellezza*

e Bizzarria, edited by Andrea Carne, in the *Times Literary Supplement* (2 May 2003), p. 9.

187 Ibid.

188 On 25 May 1975 a BBC Radio 3 programme, 'Poetry Cambridge', broadcast extracts, including Gascoyne's, but as a poem rather than a translation. Again, I am indebted to Erin O'Neill at the Written Archives Centre.

189 He died 8 January 1976; Blanche had died two years earlier to the day, 8 January 1974.

190 Reprinted in *Selected Prose 1934–1996*, p. 125. He translated another 'Mozart' poem in the notebook dated 1983–1995: 'O joy of so many years! And you magic flute ...'/ 'O joie de tant d'années! Et toi flûte enchantée ...'. (Unpublished). See **Appendix B**.

191 Introduced by Daniel Leuwers (Montpellier: Fata Morgana, 1983), pp. 51–70.

192 'Gravida' and 'A Lone Woman Asleep', op. cit., pp. 145–46. Writing of 'the case of Jouve', Auster suggests in his Introduction that Jouve's 'is a poetry without predecessors and without followers. If his work was somewhat forgotten during the period dominated by the Surrealists – which meant that recognition of Jouve's achievement was delayed almost a generation – he is now widely considered to be one of the major poets of the half-century,' p. xxxvii.

193 M. Duclos, op. cit., 'Entretien avec David Gascoyne', p. 59.

194 Similarly, in his letter of 22 April 1989 to Callander, he refers to the review in these terms: 'An impossible task adequately to summarize even the fiction in an article that length,' p. 4.

195 The transcription is mine from a cassette recording I made of the broadcast.

196 My translation of part of the final section of the letter to Dr Alan Munton, dated 3 March 1998. I'm very grateful to Xavier Guégan for his valuable help in deciphering de Bayser's handwriting and meaning in one section of this letter.

197 Op. cit., p. 12. My translation.

198 Letter dated 27 February 1988, p. 3. In his letter to Callander of 22 April 1989, he writes: I have been extremely fortunate in my life in having known not only Jouve, but also Eluard and Breton, Jules Supervielle, André Frénaud, Jean Follain, Yves Bonnefoy, Philippe Jaccottet and André du Bouchet, and translated at least a few poems by all except Bonnefoy. I admire Edmond Jabès', p. 5. Gascoyne forgot to include here amongst others, Yves de Bayser, Pierre Emmanuel, René Char, Philippe

Soupault, Bernard Delville, Eugène Guillevic, Jean Tardieu, Michel Leiris and Tristan Tarza. During the years since Gascoyne's death in 2001, I have recovered unpublished versions of poems by Henri Michaux, Jean-Paul de Dadelsen, O. V. de L. Milosz, Jean Rousselot, Gustave Roud, Alain Bosquet, Roland-Victor Lachambre, Joë Bousquet, Valéry Larbaud, Robert Desnos, Blaise Cendrars, Pierre Seghers, Roger Caillois, Max Jacob, Michel Déguy, René Guy Cadou, Georges Ribemont-Dessaignes, Lucien Scheler and Georges Schehadé.

SECTION 1

GASCOYNE'S TRANSLATIONS
OF POEMS BY JOUVE

DAVID GASCOYNE

PUBLISHED TRANSLATIONS
OF POEMS BY
PIERRE JEAN JOUVE

From S U E U R D E S A N G (1933; 1934)

Val Etrange

Gravida / *Gravida*[1]

The rocky path is sown with sombre cries
Archangels keeping guard over the gorges' weight
The naked stones beneath the twilight waves
Are emerald green with foam and blood.

How beautiful! in illustration the sad mountainside
Sings of the death but not of the warm sex of night
Which trembles as it passes endlessly away
Towards that awesome place where I have always longed to live.

There, wall and bitter frontier, smell of wood,
Of tears and manure
And the touching son trembles once more to see
How hard is what was tender when he saw it in the womb.

1 First published in *New Road* 4 (1946).

From SUEUR DE SANG

Sueur de sang

Sexe amer je ne l'ai pas vu en vain [2]

I

I not in vain beheld that bitter sex. The woman's back
In its appearance gleaming. Silence of the birds
On that day now among mild shades sunk dated down.

Miracle of the voice, O if my work endure,
Did you then rise from circumstances desert-like as these,
That did such evil to the soul, of one so pure?

Le ciel est dans l'intimité

II

The sky is intimately hid in cloudy sky
The clouds are in the water and the water in the house
The house within the heart, the latter in
Despair, but such despair within the heart
The heart inside the house, the house in space,
Space stricken with human sickness beneath the sky –

The angel of destruction sets to work; and I rejoice.

---

2 Both sections first published in *Poetry* (London), No. 11 (September– October 1947).

From S U E U R D E S A N G

Pieta

Pieta / *Une ombre maternelle tu le tiens* [3]

Maternal shadow, closely to you do you hold
His dying body on the brink of madness.
Hold him to you close. To see him still means ah!
                What rending shreds
Of sacred horror binding your softness round with love
O memory
Mindful how starkly you were destitute
And mindful of how his body out of yours,
              that body's soul,
Once was torn forth when black fires
              split across your brow.

[Fragment]

3 From Notebook 4 (*c.* 1950) in the British Library Manuscripts Department.
First published in *Selected Verse Translations* (London: Enitharmon Press, 1996).

From MATIÈRE CÉLESTE (1937)

Hélène

Woman and Earth | *La Femme et la Terre* [4]

Was stronger than the light this heart which beat in her,
Her blood to the moon's influence more open lay
Than lifeblood shed; her night was denser and more hirsute than
The Night, and just as sparkling and as hard –
More sex than soul a star more than a sex
Temple with tresses drifting from the dome

Are sleeping now that other granite, roses overblown
That pass away and vanish in the light's pure lake –
Old weakness felt no more, all distance done away:
O lofty lofty lands and alien azure sky
Weigh down on her who now is no more known
As bosom or as spasm or as hot tears spilt in Time:
Who underneath the ground has turned right round
To face another, a more ashen sun.

4 First published in *Kingdom Come*, Vol. 3, No. 9 (November–December 1941), then in *New Directions* 7 (USA 1942), and in David Gascoyne's *Poems 1937–42* (1943).

From MATIÈRE CÉLESTE

Matière céleste

The Moths | *Les Papillons* [5]

There are moths shut-in below
Moths pink and black and plump
Such moths are warm with an inhuman glow
Their wings are faults of memory
These creatures have the accent of two faces marked by fate
When they are hanging strictly folded-up below.
When the moths of the flesh below are called
Up from the shadows where they wait
They rise up pink and plump
They rise up but they flap
They flap but soon are swollen tight
With odour, blindness, nudity and weight.

[5] First published in *Poetry* (London), Vol. 1, No. 5 (March–April 1941).

From MATIÈRE CÉLESTE

Matière céleste

Brow | Front[6]

The sun's come back upon the window-panes
The birds make song
And Hope invades the window-panes
Of golden-fired insurgent Morn.
Revolutions make dank mansions shake
While in the gracious light the Heroes march
And down across the blue roofs the bared heads
Of families of remorseless tyrants fall –

When Man bound to his evil fate
Is dead
Struck down by the myriad blows that he so well deserved
Behold his brow take form in the calm blue on high!

6 First published in *New Directions* 7 (USA 1942), then in *Poems 1937–42* (1943).

From MATIÈRE CÉLESTE

Nada

Nada / *Les gloires les plus belles* [7]

The most beautiful most naked and most tragic splendours
The oppositions between suns and darknesses
In night's forever black protective space
The deepest ecstasy in unknown arms

All things that are no more
And yet are born in agony at dawn
See thee and lift thee up ineffable uproar
Innumerable flaming fireless sex of stars

Love's flame too flaming and too crucified
Upon the intimate blackness of our eyes
Desert of love
Organ of God.

[7] First published in *Delta*, 3me année, No. 1 (Easter 1939), then in *New Directions*
7 (USA 1942), and in *Poems 1937–42* (1943).

From MATIÈRE CÉLESTE

Nada

The Desires of the Flesh are a Desire for Death /
Le désir de la chair est désir de la mort [8]

The desires of the flesh are a desire for death
And the desire for flight is earthly, of the earth
The love of gold is the great cities' excrement
Desires of youth are all a greed for graves

As hard some hungers are as a woman's nakedness
I make love on the daily bed I lie in pain
Drowsy with light the pearls of morn lie strewn
Along death's green-marged shore

O, it was not in vain that Christ's sweet saints
Did with the devil wage long bitter war
Nor is it all in vain that Christ's and the devil's breasts
Are made to seem one and the same in this deep night

O take account but of the tears' weight, not
For their own sake, but for the voids they leave behind
And sliding in black vertigo down the sheer sides of this
Obliterated world: draw nigh, draw nigh unto the One.

8 First published in *New Road* 4 (1946).

From MATIÈRE CÉLESTE

Hélène

A Lone Woman Asleep / *Une seule femme endormie* [9]

When there came days sunk deep in damp your beauty seemed
 increased
And ever warmer grew your glow when rain fell in despair
And when days came that were like deserts you
Grew moister than the trees in the aquarium of time
And when the ugly anger of the world raged in our hearts
And sadness lisped exhausted through the leaves
You became as sweet as death
Sweet as teeth in the ivory skull-box of the dead
And pure as the skein of blood
Your laughter made to trickle down from your soul's parted lips
When there come days deep-sunk and damp the world grows still
 more dark
When days like deserts come, the heart is drenched with tears.

9 First published in *New Road* 4 (1946).

From MATIÈRE CÉLESTE

Hélène

In Helen's Land / *La-bas dépôt tombé du ciel* [10]

Like some deposit dropped from a mystic sky
Yonder intones an organ hewn of rock: which leaning, pores
Over the rain's grey shadow as though over its own thought;
But what is in its heart? There Helen lies.

This is the shattered rock of Helen's majesty and state
Which rules over that uterine deep land
Wherein her milkwhite flesh had life; and where
She met her death, in splendour, sick with love, adorned with flowers,

Where naked forests trembled at her breath.

10 First published in David Gascoyne's *Selected Poems* (London: Enitharmon Press, 1994).

From MATIÈRE CÉLESTE

Hélène

[Untitled] / *Tempo di Mozart* [11]

Here the sky, the vast sky is full of gusts of wind and rock
O harden the sky blue rock and make the rock's air quiver
How steely sounds the singing of the antique violin's strings
How gentle feels the stroking of the genius's green heart

How precious is the rock with its mounds of unburnt ash
How pure, how out of season is the great mass of gold!
How chilly feels the fervour slipping into the lips below
Of the inviolable hymen of the day.

Translated by David Gascoyne and Roger Scott

11 This fragment is a later translation of the first two stanzas of 'Tempo di Mozart', the first complete version of which appeared, as indicated earlier, in *Adam International Review*, No. 422/424 (1980).

From K Y R I E

Transpierce me Lord with my own Grief /
Pénètre-moi Seigneur de ma propre douleur [12]

Transpierce me Lord with my own grief
Give work to the machinery of my tears
Remove from me my last repose
And drive me from my knowledge, Pitiless One

Soul! filled with music O surround
My ugliness unceasingly like an erotic shade
Giving direction to my pains

O pensive Soul of God
Silent when I cried out in hunger or joy
Most beautiful (and to be dealer to me of my death)

Suave eucharist
To be devoured by my mouth's bloodless lips
Thou knowest how in blindness I pray unto thee
O wounded side death can no more corrupt

The deeper sin, the more truthful the light
And higher like a flag on high
Torn but resplendent from its black
Worn backward-leaning flagstaff knowledge flies.

12 First published in *New Road* 4 (1946).

From K Y R I E (1938)

Les Quatre Cavaliers

The Two Witnesses / *Les Deux Témoins* [13]

Have pity, O harsh Lamb upon these last two
Witnesses who shall in scarlet cloak be slain and have no tomb
And take O Liberty into thy charge their red remains
For these are the two holy candle-bearers of the Lord
For they have been given power to shut the sky
For their mouths' fire has quite consumed the unjust man
For they have turned the waters into blood
But at last the Beast of the abyss
Has been sent power to deliver them
Has made war and has killed them and all their deeds has undone.

13 First published in *New Directions* 7 (USA 1942), then in *Poems 1937–42* (1943).

From K Y R I E

Nul N'En Etait Témoin
Austère nudité de l'érotique Hélène [14]

Austere nudity of the erotic Helen
Thou my prayer in stone and wind
Smile and insult through the rending veil
Woman too greatly beautiful beyond the passing years
Mourning memory green grass.

14 First published in *New Road* 4 (1946).

From K Y R I E

Insula Monti Majoris | *Ces roches qu'elles étaient tendres sur les marais* [15]

How tender were the rocks upon the marsh
How hard the rocks were in the rock

How the birds climbed in the eternal sky
How the winds swung to and fro
The summer earth's black essences

How violently those suns beat down upon the plague
How frightened were those hearts
To be deprived of woman's sex
How deeply slept the shadows in the shadow of the stones

How holy was the terror of the day
Around the sounding stone
Their stony modulation was without fault
They sang

How sepulchral and giant was their soul
That God had pierced with a wound greater than the soul!
How far had they gone out from woman's womb
And how the odour became sweet out of their tombs!

How black were those white men against the fine day's light
Sleeping yet never asleep
For the Master was in agony always
Until the end of time beneath the glowing sky.

15 First published in *Folios of New Writing* (Spring 1940), then in *New Directions* 7 (USA 1942).

From DEFENCE ET ILLUSTRATION (1943)

Freedom or Death / *La Liberté ou la mort* [16]

I see it once again, in rather a sombre, a windless corner, tight-stretched and unwrinkled by any fold. The stuff it was made of was softest silk, which seemed to make a profound, suave, unsounding music; consisting of three cruelly torn pieces, each seeming enlarged by the (two) others.

That which first made my *heart stand still* was the crimson piece; not crimson though, no, rose-red, as of a rose with crushed and dried up petals; yet rose-blossom red, did I say? not so; but in a sort of anguish verging on lilac, of a graver tone, that exquisite tone that the assassinated victim's blood has acquired at last, the blood of Marat.

16 First published in *Selected Verse Translations* (London: Enitharmon Press, 1996), edited by Alan Clodd & Robin Skelton, with an introductory essay by Roger Scott. From Add. MS56045 in the British Library Manuscripts Department.

From LA VIERGE DE PARIS (1946)

Résurrection des morts

The Resurrection of the Dead / *Le sang humain, l'espoir, le souvenir humain* [17]

Man's blood, and hope, and human memory
From the black-tinged ingredients of space
That Daniel's lion-den beneath the smouldering eye
The blue hole of the heavenly throne

The great skies have been raised up like high walls
The black of cracks is outlined by the bluish sheen of steel
The millions of the judgment called, like planets all too pale
With memories of underneath the earth, go flying past

And the harlot seated high upon the waters, and
Downfallen, the great death poured from the cups
And I have seen what blows the heavenly host endures
And the white giant who has a dagger in his mouth

I've seen the only liberty there is vanquished by death
Beneath the swaddling-linen of the sky
Bathed in the black blood of the cups and wounds
When the great harlot of the waters had burst into flame

I was a man; O now illumine my remains!
And grant me pardon if I lived but for a Beast
And if I was voluptuously in love with lovely Death,
I was the poet: O illumine the whole

And if thou wast not God I will establish still
On Nothing over Nothingness the soul's supremacy,
For God not of the dead but of the living is the God
And no more can they die, the risen dead.

17 First published in *Folios of New Writing* (Spring 1940), then in *New Directions 7* (USA 1942).

From LA VIERGE DE PARIS

Résurrection des morts

When Glory's Spring Returns / *Au Printemps de la gloire* [18]

The sun sheds its incandescence on the new-sprung shoots,
A sun no eyes ever beheld, there were none pure enough –
Sun rearisen after the combustion of long death.
The Spring of ancient glories is all crystal and fresh air
And the works of the great masters – Dante, Virgil – now appear
As sacred garments that adorn the naked outward form
In which they walk abroad. One may perceive
As with miraculous candour the child Baudelaire shewed forth
And Delacroix and Courbet from their tents of light emerged
To reassume eternally their golden fleece of dream.
From high savannahs of the air Rimbaud smiles down at last.

18 First published in *Poetry* (London), No. 11 (September-October 1947).

From LA VIERGE DE PARIS

Prière du soir

Evening Prayer / *O mon dieu, toute éternité de mon amour* [19]

O Thou to all eternity God of my love,
My prayer beholds Thee in this silence dense and dark
Whereunto I after yet one more day am come:
Sacred the dark, wretched the ragged wound,
Wound wedded to the darkness and with peace welded as one.
O God, Thou art substantial made through Thy rebirth by night,
Out of Thy absence, from that grievous wound no less;
Thou art as the pure void and all else emptiness is blind,
Thou art the lamb of jet-black fleece whereon clear may the brand
Of death be read, though letterless; and now allow the wound
To close, as closely the soft curtains to be drawn that shelter hope.

---

19 First published in *Selected Poems* (London: Enitharmon Press, 1994).

From GENIE (1948)

Siegl

Le doux rire d'Hélène arrive par la vitre [20]

Helen's sweet laughter pierces the panes to reach
The solid wall upon the heights; and the cold lakes
Weep joyful tears for a hundred acts of love and shame
Of transport and desire over those most strange plants
Sent here in memory of her, at the pure hour
When warming 'neath the sensual velvet of another sky
Aurora combing her gold hair beckoning her towards death.

20 From Notebook 3 (c. 1950) in the British Library Manuscripts Department. First published in *Selected Verse Translations* (London: Enitharmon Press, 1996).

From D I A D È M E (1949)

Ciels

To Himself / *A Soi-Même* [21]

Write now only for the sky
Write for the curved arc of the sky
And to no black letter of lead
Resort to wrap thy writing in
Write for the odour and the breath
Write for the sheet of silver leaf
Let no unlovely human face

Have glimpse or knowledge or rumour thereof
Write for the god and for the fire
Write for the sake of a beloved place
And may nothing to do with man intrude.

21 From Notebook 3 (*c.* 1950) in the British Library Manuscripts Department.
First published in *Selected Verse Translations* (London: Enitharmon Press, 1996).

From L A N G U E (1954)[22]

I

Dans cette saison où inuait le monde informe et dernier

During the moulting season of the formless final world
The conquerors held out still: alone and without horses either of
    plaster or of gold
And without money (lost in the sands and in the circuses, and on all
    fronts)
Without even a moist lance's oriflamme. And then what thrusts
    of troops that never moved!
Pure conquerors of ancient time – and all cathedrals in their train –
They awaited with their passion in the swarming towns of dwarfs
An extraordinary onslaught of empty emotion and explosiveness
Which might enable all to be recovered by the vitals that were losing
    all their blood.

II

Ah! Le poète écrit pour le vide des cieux

Ah! the poet writes only for the heavens' empty space
    Pure blue that winter can no longer see! he writes in conjuration of
    the silence of the snows
Of the stifling of fallacious festal days! and in the lack and in the
    lacklustre it reveals, each line he writes is just as though he were
    not there (and his slim figure, dressed as a matador, is just as
    though he were not there),
And in his solitude devoted to that admirable, secret conjuration,
    behold him pleading his peculiar loves
When none would undertake to risk love's courage in his stead:

Then on the fabled winds' black shore, over the seaweeds' slumber,
    under nearly weightless whirling swells of fog,
He seals the word up in the bottle of green glass,
Bells of despair and horrible seawrack!
He launches on the highest wave a bottle without action, force or
    aim, yet which one day
The waves will wash up to love's level, beyond beauty, beyond
    glory, beyond day.

III
Jour claire!! Reprends ton dillon sur les avenues mortelles

Clear light of day! flow once more through the furrow you have
    worn upon the mortal avenues,
Gleam on the capitals and globes of stone, waken the sacred snakes,
All men's activities! And mortal thought of mine pursue once more
Your way towards hope's narrow zone, with great deliberate works
    in view:
Both works and death before my eyes stand like glad monuments
    devoured by the sky's plants,
Pure ruin well contented to be filled with its vast future and its natural
    love.

22 First published in the *London Magazine*, Vol. 2, No. 2 (February 1955).

DAVID GASCOYNE

UNCOLLECTED TRANSLATIONS
FROM THE FRENCH OF
PIERRE JEAN JOUVE

From SUEUR DE SANG (1933; 1934)

Les Masques

Le désespoir a des ailes

Despair has wings
Love has despair
For shimmering wing
Societies can change

From S U E U R D E S A N G (1933; 1934) [23]

Crachats

Spittle on the asphalt has always made me think
Of the face painted on the veil of holy women.

23 First appearance in the *Encrages* article, op. cit.

Hélène

Mozart

The sky the vast sky of wind breaths and stone
Stone of azure harden and tremble air of rock
What steel sings in the ancient violins
How caressing are the green genius's hearts

How precious is the stone with the mounts of ash
How pure! unseasonable, the gold's volume
How cold the ardour in its folds
Inviolable hymen of the day

The earth would thrust its breast into justice's domain
The azure, azure, azure! would perish tender and blue.

But the hour just as in a drama of glances inter-changed
Like a virgin's mother violating love
Like the poisonous flesh of flowers of the field
Or great as was Christ's passion in the dark
Has changed.

Heavenly hurricane held back by an edge
The void is hung on the edges of your eyes
Male hurricane! All is lost, all is calm
All is white all is dying but dazzling bright
With what is passing across the suffering of your eyes
All collapses into naked springs of tears,
Falls silent, and in the silence angels keep
The most precious pale surrender is fulfilled.

I am he who loves
Child whose swaddling clothes are now spread out
In clouds in insights of the soul and prayers
Child whose eyes were pierced by rays
Child of amorous wrath
While I was shutting my own grown man's eyes.

24 The four poems on the theme of Mozart were first published in *Adam International Review*, No. 422–24 (1980), pp. 48–9. English versions only.

From MATIÈRE CÉLESTE

Kyrie

In the Common Grave | *Mozart dans la fosse commune*

Sobbing bleeding smiling thunderclap
And the cherubim's swords enflamed therein
Here lies at rest a song of stark perfection
Genius! Unfolds a love vaster than incense is
More beautiful even than the universe
More sensitive than God who first created it Himself.

From MATIÈRE CÉLESTE

Nada

Viaticum / *Viaticum* (Mozart)

Death's extraordinary terrors
Will be borne by an angel's wavering
The agonies of the head's
Compression and the relinquishing of all flowers or tears
Will be borne away in an angel's sob
The battles of the dark be glorified
In such a silence that you go forward pure
Unwavering genius
The words and the song will be no longer flesh but blood
The sun will be no longer orb but flower of blood
The soul will be no more, a new-born church
Of blood will then find out its own nether abode.

From MATIÈRE CÉLESTE

Nul n'en était témoin

Don Juan / *Don Juan*

I listen to you O so deeply profound Song – come back
From the realm of the powerful dead
Having endured the loss of flesh and every work
Having lost the white genius with the sombre phallus
Having clasped the hand of the Stone Guest.

O genius sweet Child, pity my wretchedness!
I've searched for you among the blackest floods.

I believe that your dawn is more beautiful, my eyes
Go further, that the spell is stronger, that sex
Is darker and death's brilliance greater
To the old bones in the sorcerous cemeteries
Brought back by the mountain – and that my woe
Is great – that the light of the great secret things
With the painted heroes of life and death
Has in my heart at least been manifested and said
When the hand of the Stone Guest held my own.

From LANGUE III (1954) [25]

A tant d'années de la naissance, à quelques journées

At so many years' distance from the day of birth, with death distant by only a few days, after so many figures that appeared to rise and fall in the same sky of desire wherein disappointment and pleasure were both of the same shade of blue, after all the monotony befallen in the gardens – the distance that seemed so close at hand yet so remotely lost – and all the insecurity of the end – art in its repetitions altogether terrified to be alone amidst unbounded and bare space, one seeks the meaning and the letter and the spirit: the meaning is dear to God: the meaning is what reaches the God-consciousness, and as a phrase resounds from the main vocable and rings through all the rest that are disposed on either side of it, the word of life is only to be read in the absurd – imprinted within absolute Absurdity and shining there like love of which the forms are infinite.

25 First published in 'A New Poem by Pierre Jean Jouve: "Language"', in the London Magazine, Vol. 2, No. 2 (February 1955), pp. 49-52, and reprinted in Selected Prose 1934–1996, edited by Roger Scott (London: Enitharmon Press, 1998). Unaccountably, this translation was not included in either the Collected Verse Translations (Oxford University Press, 1970) or the Selected Verse Translations (London: Enitharmon 1996).

DAVID GASCOYNE

UNPUBLISHED DRAFT
TRANSLATIONS OF POEMS
BY PIERRE JEAN JOUVE

From LES NOCES (1931) [26]

Noces

Young Spirit / *L'Esprit Jeune*

The trees whose height the eye takes in are blue with joy
The earth whose contours the eye follows has an intense
                                                    ruddy hue
The sky when it is glimpsed appears a pink or lilac blue;
The plumy grasses flow and plunge like ocean waves
We feel press down on us the unseen power
The spirits who dwell behind the wind send up their
                                                    prayer
From chimneys spirals of adoring smoke ascend;
The music of contemplation seizes the birds
And the dilating soul is caught away up beyond space
Far beyond conceptions and higher even than love.

26 One of three previously unpublished translations of poems by Jouve which Gascoyne contributed to John Lehmann's Third Programme poetry series, *New Soundings*, 12, broadcast on 11 March 1953. This poem, included in the original script, was cut from the recording. The other two, 'Par contre, Paysage' / 'Landscape in Another Direction' and 'Paysage Intérieur' / 'Interior Landscape' (see below), were read by John Glen.

From SUEUR DE SANG (1933; 1934)

Les Masques:

P

When I was born appeared this strange white sign
That now I keep on seeing under every downcast sky
The swaddling cloth that was divided at my birth
Was stamped on the right with shadow marks
that spelt the word 'Welcome'
And upon the left appeared the letter P
Standing for Pity towards everyone.

[British Library, Add. MS71704E]

From SUEUR DE SANG (1933; 1934)

Sueur de sang

Landscape in another direction / *Par Contre, Paysage*

The pathways winding through the largest woods lead on
                                        the soul
And out at last across the calm of terraces of sward
Towards the mist-wrapped mountains in the gaps of which
                                        there sleep
Temples standing on guard over the dead in their old tombs.

Far-off, old memories glow like gold in the smouldering coals
Of the heroic days gone by. Oh innocent highland places
Oh smiling temples and you towns, scenes hovering in the blue.

From MATIÈRE CÉLESTE (1937):

Nada

Darkness / *Ténèbres*

Pity upon the naked god within our darkness dying
But no pity upon
Him who would have our flesh of darkness taken
And would have taken us in sin back to the dark
And added yet more darkness to our sin! And carried us
On still more torture-swollen waves of blood
Back to be then brought back at the dead stroke of dark
To life, so that the filtered darkness sacrificed in him
Might change, through death's travail like worm's work
                                 in the heart,
Today breaking on our soul with so celestial a blue
As yet it cannot know, for only death can show our soul
                                 such sky.

[British Library, Add. MS71704H]

From MATIÈRE CÉLESTE

He is far more than a prince, for he's a man.

Sarastro in The Magic Flute

O joy of so many years! And you magic flute
Re-echo one more day upon the secret surge
Bathe the primal love
Grant us the pledge
Out of the church tombs
Make those old black rituals laughing blaze
But cure us of the iron and of the drunk substances
Which with a dead horizon conceal the primal love.

[From a Notebook dated '1983–1995']²⁷

27 It is clear from the notebook that Gascoyne intended, too, to work on versions of two other Mozart poems: 'Dernier signe à Salzbourg' and 'Sanctus à Salzbourg'; he had copied out both in the original French, and had translated half of the second: see below. Jouve's 'Un Tableau de Balthus' is on a later page.

From K Y R I E (1938)

Kyrie

Interior Landscape / *Paysage intérieur*

Against the trees the golden blue sky strikes
And shadows of the eyes' pupils are cast upon the trees
The trees are of gigantic size, the temples' columns stand
Like perfect teeth upon their rocky shelf
The river's flow bears down with it the sands it cherishes
The depths by recollection are relieved
The mighty pillars of poetry form towns
Evening sinks and solidifies about men's mortal limbs
A mourning girl goes gathering into her aproned gown
The scattered ashes of the man she loved.

The suns you hold between the folds of your titanic thighs
Shine with as hard a radiance as they once had in kings' tombs
Their heavy-weighing majesty fulfils the function of
The human column and draws up all but the drops
Of grief's salt water (for the oneness of the sky
Could never reach the depths of any vessel so profound).

From K Y R I E

Kyrie

Sanctus à Salzbourg

O terribly dark master of the deed / exploit
Magic leaf of summer fallen back
On the memory of my <u>corroded</u> departed
Smile without end sculpture and cemetery
O terribly true master of my exploit
Light's tireless sigh
Mass of choirs mass of the summer sky
Mass of [...]

[Unfinished 1st draft from a notebook dated '1983–1995']

From LA VIERGE DE PARIS (1946)

Nuit des Saints

A cup stands silent on the table
Manuscripts lie signifying rings
The walls are as chaste as are white walls
Here the prisoner draws his hourly breath

Nothing would be prisoner if all
Were dead under his hand and the whole desert sky
Around him always were other than the way
[*last line missing*]

From H Y M N E I (1947)

Plaine des Renards[28]

Green is the waveswept plain at the hour of the budding corn
Green are three windswept trees, green the pensive/thoughtful hope
Green is the sleeping wood that winds across the scene
Green are the ditches, and the soul, O vast scope of my eyes

Green and the grey of scar and the limpid wrath
Of the sky above, and for ever the gentle kindness quiet
The rooks fly off/move away towards the stern horizon's rim
Where presently the huge smokes of the city shall appear.

28 I have transcribed the English draft from a page in Gascoyne's 'Common-place Notebook (1948)' in the Beinecke Rare Book and Manuscript Library, Yale University.

From GENIE (1948)

Seigl

Chemin des artistes

'Green waters! If the rocks tumble tragically down
In harmony with the return of love's embrace
With darkness and if the weather grieve a sparse-
                                        treed wood
With feathers and with acid; and the antique light
To see the wandering weightless cumulus clouds
                                        begins to laugh;
With the irritating ceaseless simoom[29] arise
And then the grass fringe round the pool's edge is
                        blown back leaving it bare...'

And the nymph whose eyes reflected this lone
                                        paradise replied:
'Rather see here how in the distant gulley rise
Enormous silvered masses overshadowing the trees
The blood of the jagged shadowed valley that the
                                        painter haunts,
~~The rock-falls that torment the mason's fanshaped~~
                                        ~~yard~~
And in their souls the wounded warriors' lament?
Primaeval love lying in a naked beauty.'

[Incomplete preliminary draft. British Library, Add. MS71704D]

29 Editor's note: 'Strong, suffocating sand-laden wind of the deserts of Arabia
and North Africa', according to the *Collins English Dictionary* (3rd edition, 1992).
'Le vent' in Jouve's text.

From D I A D È M E (1949)

La Main de Dieu

Dragon Intérieur

I sit aimlessly waiting in the ante-room
Of death. Thou hast done injury to my soul
Adversity of countless coils and jaws of gold
Rings wrapped in smoke and twisted wings
And loathsome fuzz

Long bristling of the force of nothingness
Over the ancient lands the gates of decadence
Long sigh. But o thou dragon navigating
Across the sky since childhood's graceless days

Art thou not the daydream of the sky?
Yet art thou not the reason for the dawn
And I not guilty O thou rainbow-face
Of the serpent that adores?

[British Library, Add. MS70714G, 1950]

From D I A D È M E

Of a Town / *D'une Ville*

A red object enamelled green
Enamel of blood-red of plants of tears
Over illustrious canals of magical density
Where frantic towers raise up their weapon-like beauties
                                        to the sky
And grassy silences reign over the old bodies strewn about

Magical effects of blackened green of old green of green green
Velvets coloured like Christ's precious blood and charms
Of crypts exalted by their hoard of pious corpse
Spanish sunlight lighting a unique kind of brick
And musical effusions as of bridges and warm angels

Of murders and of love intrigues the aged residue.

[British Library, Add. MS71704G, 1950]

From D I A D È M E

La Main de Dieu

Rabbouni

And Christ appeared to Mary in the guise
Of a gardener, she just then saw
The empty tomb in which angels or shades
Seemed like her grief as dusty as that shrine

And with her tears still dripping from her cheeks
                              upon her breast
Just then her glistening eye was struck by a man's form
'Where hast thou laid him, gardener,' she asked
That I may go and bring back his remains

And lay them here again?' And the man spoke but one
                                                    word
Mary, so far-away so broken and so robbed of life

That she dropped to the ground and heard him say
Do not touch me. O Master! O Rabbouni!

[British Library, Add. MS71704D, 1944–1950]

From D I A D È M E

La Main de Dieu

Les Plantes de la Solitude

Solitude has its own strange way
Of mirroring as in a frozen marsh
Defeat arising out of victory
The doubt by bleeding thigh clearly disclosed

And strange proliferating seedy grass
Embraces blue on spring cactuses
Vivid rose leaning towards the dahlias inert
In the glare of the massive, nude and stuporific sun

And countless anxious pangs that matter (Nature) feels
Devoured by insects' pious hordes
The coloured fibres: tranquil destitute
Is death's slow last extremity in this abandoned place.

[British Library, Add. MS71704D, 1944–1950]

From D I A D È M E

La Main de Dieu

Que veut le dragon? [30]

What does the dragon want? that I be fond of him
His moving is around about the sky
Within the bowl's furthermost depths
With all his thousandfold ancient degrees

His tears his hesitating stays
And his red mouths of flame
And it is not till he has uttered I want
To the cloudy dark, the mire, the [*squalid*]

And not till he has said I am
Out of his eyes that look like an old crone's
That wisdom has no longer any [*door*]
Against haggard kindheartedness

But it is when he cries I am ashamed
(The tears the hesitating stays)
That man goes rushing back to any shame
To give his passion its old sway again.

[British Library, Add. MS71704D]

---

30 Unrevised. French original in 1st edition of *Diadème* (1949), but not
collected in Jouve's *Oeuvre* I (1987).

From DIADÈME

La Main de Dieu

Thoughts of the Reign / *Pensées du règne*

Give me the wherewithal to create the imaginable sky
That has nothing in common with the soft sources of air
The great blond stretch of hair senseless with [*pleasure*]
About heavy coloured lips from which
The whole earth is perfumed and to conceive [...]

[Fragment British Library, Add. MS71704D]

127

From O D E (1950)

Trombes

Beneath the great spread table of the sea the hills'
                         [*worn-out 'trombes'*]
Are repeated by the grief and the green misty embraces
Of the breasts full of male power in the black and diamond-
                            studded sky
Alack-a-day! and well-a-day! And the etherized thunderbolts
                              of morn
Wounding wound of the eye, roll the thick ~~wrappings~~
Round the circuit, funereal quietness, of two diamond-
                            studded eagles.

[Fragment British Library, Add. MS71704E]

From O D E

Nuits 1

Hear how on the wind that ruffles the striped fleece of
                              the thinnest cloud
Comes the song of the nightingale or Queen of the night
From her throat swollen with [balmy] roses' perfume
slowly swims from the open sea of blackness, the cry
Of the nocturnal jasmine and the purplish tinted skin
Of the secretly killed creatures of the shades: night murder
And the stars' slow sobbing afterwards: night blood
Hear the fierce trills of the charming queen of death
Triumphantly break into small shining spots across the
                              slumberer's wake.

What is your will, malignant goddess?
Where are your berry-smooth green blushing breasts
Where your belly split by Eros's brown stain
And the places dulled by opiate's sweetish breath
In the tranquillity of hell? O malign creature
Where do you take your fitful pleasure on the carpet of
                              blue-lidded kisses?
Can you not salvage my lust out of the [*lurking*]well-policed
                              dusk?
Can you not once bring back clear daylight, make it shine on
all my loops and islets, all my heads and (armpits) [*groins?*]
Before death fetches me away? […]

[Fragment, unrevised. British Library, Add. MS71704E]

From P R I È R E (1924)

Esprits

Guide

This quite transparent man
His eyes
Clearest of wellsprings,
His lips
Burnt by the light of classic suns, disclosing
                                        perfect teeth,
His twenty-year-old smile
In a noble face the skin of which
Had been stretched across its bone by heaven's hand!
His soul
Oh who has glimpsed his soul
Swift-footed, melancholy, disdainful and naive?
Soul of true knowledge, he hides it away,
A smiling word,
Is his reply,
A friendly wink
His self-protection,
Confidence is tight around him like a belt of rope,
And his body is [*line incomplete*]
Man of the sky, what secret do you keep! Tell us why
                                        you are on your guard!
But he smiles, his teeth are a twenty-year-old's, and his
Language is not one I understand.

[British Library, Add. MS71704D, 1944–1950]

Eternité ravie et verte [31]

Time
For the eternity of light with open lips

Time in which rare youth's high hills are fixed
in their setting of sky as a lucid fixed idea would be set off by
a sapphire
Beyond the tiny agitation of death and history
in the forecourt of memory's temple
(Far from the symphonies of tumbling silver upon the
black woodlands of poetry wherein the loved one dwelt and close
beside the gulf wherein the valleys' [******] from the crystal waters
at the [very] spot where every day the furious breezes are reborn)
The eternity of light with open lips
Sensitive to the green pineneedles sighing and the lifeless shiver
of moiré;
Time of the blue planes of desire, time of the green
      planes of the sapphire ...

[Fragment. Published in *Mercure de France*, No. 1082 (1 October 1953), pp. 193–201].[32]

31 McFarlin Library, University of Tulsa. Uncollected: not included in Jouve's *Oeuvre* I (Paris: Mercure de France, 1987).
32 What follows is the only example I have found of an exasperated, critical response by Gascoyne to Jouve. 'Oh no, it's no use pretending one can adequately translate this sort of writing What has happened to Pierre's later poetry? There seems to be a predominance of aesthetic and sometimes empty repetitive decorative elements, a certain byzantism, a certain parnassian allure and Claudelian *envergure*, that in the end result in large splendidly hung panels suspended in space around a diminutive cluster of genuine motivating symbols – meaning: fear of death, nostalgia for the exaltation of furiously squandered libido, intermittent recollection of the true peace that passeth understanding,– tragic awareness of man increasingly uninterested in his true condition. Man seems to [have] a partial individual momentary view, to be ever more careless of whether or not what happens to him means something permanent and coherent [...].' D.G.

SECTION TWO

GASCOYNE'S TRANSLATIONS OF ESSAYS BY JOUVE AND GROETHUYSEN

The Unconscious, Spirituality, Catastrophe (Jouve)
The Present Greatness of Mozart (Jouve)
Preface to *Poèmes de la folie de Hölderlin* (Groethuysen)

Pierre Jean Jouve

THE UNCONSCIOUS, SPIRITUALITY, CATASTROPHE

Translated by David Gascoyne

We have to-day in our possession the knowledge of thousands of worlds (to conceal which was until recently man's most constant effort) within the world of Man; knowledge of the thousands of strata in the psychic geology of that terrible being who obstinately – marvellously, perhaps (although never succeeding conclusively) – emerges by degrees out of black muddy depths and the womb's blood. Channels and passageways have sprung open within him with a complexity and a rapidity that are almost frightening. This being, Man, is not, as was formerly supposed, a personage attired in suit or uniform; rather is he as it were a dolorous abyss, closed in, yet almost open – a colony of insatiable, seldom contented forces, circling clumsily around like a swarm of crabs and ever on the alert against attack. And further, in Man's heart and in the womb of his intelligence we are now able to perceive so many suckers and voracious mouths, so much cherished or abominated faecal matter, so cannibalistic an appetite, and incestuous fantasies so strange and so tenacious, and withal so strong a rooted tendency towards the obscene, and such prodigious accumulations of magical virtue – finally, so monstrous a Desire, alternating with so implacable an executioner – that the problem of Man seems from henceforth destined to remain forever insoluble; for after having asked ourselves how it can be possible for these depths to remain ever hidden from view, and how it can have been possible for Man to continue for so long to ignore them, we come to ask: how can it be that Man has succeeded in setting up rational consciousness against forces so determined and redoubtable? Though the world be shaken by the most violent denials, modern man nevertheless has discovered the unconscious and its structure; in it he has seen the erotic instinct and the death instinct inextricably locked together; and the face of the world of the Fault, which is to say of the world of Man, has been permanently altered by this discovery. The relationship between guilt – the fundamental feeling in all men's hearts – and the initial inter-union of the two chief instincts, can from now on be unlinked no more. Never again can we forget that we represent an insoluble *conflict* between two lines, of which one indicates the natural warmth of the creature, the other, the rational development of the person; or that there must ever remain the possibility that starting from this conflict an intimate disturbance may at any moment break out (for great were the efforts that had to be expended before we were able to succeed in resisting animal determination) and proceed to endanger the inner life. Incalculable is the extension of our sense of the tragic that is brought us by metapsychology, and even more incalculable the extension of the knowledge gained by that eye which gazes into our secret parts – which eye is none other than our own.

No longer is it to our astonishment that we are able to pass, by means of this eye, down pipes and cylinders, through unexplored ruins and vaults; able to see the face change its flesh, and destiny assume another name, desire enter the category of natural causes, and death go about its secret work. Whatever takes place between the leaden and mysterious figures who people the region of our origins, does so instantaneously, with terrible intensity, irrevocably and forever. The universe, in the person of Mr Smith, is that power which seeks to become steadily balanced until the moment comes for it to give way to its own breakdown and abandon him. The gods and all the myths form a part of this reality and they also help to build up his gigantic palace of cards. The inhuman density of all this would be enough to make his head burst open (to *alienate* him from himself) were he not of a *frivolous* (or if you prefer, intelligent) disposition, and always prepared not to see anything such as might offend him. Yet still does man goad himself onwards into battle, on into the abyss, and under certain unusual circumstances, he does achieve conscious thought. If he can manage to avoid being reduced to a sort of death by the preliminary workings of the psychic mechanism, he is able to think. It is at this point that a miracle, never so far from man as to be beyond his reach, begins to take place. Here we assist at the mystery *of sublimation*, to employ the word to which Freud has assigned so dynamic a significance. This function, by transferring energy into a given tendency, can cause the latter to cease to resemble what it was to begin with, yet without thereby severing it from its origin; to become increasingly free from the determination of necessity, and thus able to rise to higher levels. The libido would appear to be capable of vast transformations, both of quantity and of kind; capable also even of *inventing* its own particular quality, and finally, of transcending itself. This theory is a quite satisfactory one, and I cannot see that the 'soul' of man is in any way diminished by it. To the contrary, in fact. (Man to-day is greater, did he but realize it, than during the Middle Ages or the sixteenth century, both of which were periods when he held quite a high opinion of himself; just because to-day, having been injured through his narcissism, he could if he wished have access to hitherto unforeseen reserves of power.) In revealing the demonic life of the instincts, modern psychology, the aim of which is to revolutionize a diseased civilization, brings to light at the same time a new and sounder Reason.

The notion has already been put forward that it might be possible for a certain type of mind (the mystic) to maintain a fundamental relationship and agreement between the super-ego (archaic repressive force) and that more universal underlying erotic basis constituting the id (individual not-self); so that the war waged, on the level of the unconscious, by this type's super-ego against the erotic not-self, would no longer be liable to produce illness or misadventure, as often happens in ordinary cases, but would lead to an unlimited, all round increase of *depth*. This theory, on account of its dialectical implications, seems to me to be of the highest importance. If it is true, it would appear to follow that there can also exist a psychological type capable of deriving secret power from the universal unconscious (more remote than the individual unconscious), with which, by employing certain forms of discipline, this type may establish communication, and from which they may receive as much as they contribute to it – a process of exchange that can hardly be regarded as being of any but a spiritual nature. Since we must now consider the human psychic mechanism to be all-inclusive in its formation, we might almost conjecture, although still far from knowing what it is that separates the most universal unconscious tendencies from what are regarded as the loftiest spiritual impulses – a certain eroticism, as has been and will again be frequently remarked, impregnates the sublime acts of the saints – that the series of the phenomena is circular, and that in the case of the specially privileged type the lowest manifestations of the subject's nature are as though joined by an immediate inner connection to the most lofty.

Something of this sort is to be affirmed, at any rate, concerning that more humble thing which is Poetry. The poets who since Rimbaud have striven to free poetry from the restriction of the rational are well aware (even though some of them may not fully realize it) that in the unconscious (or rather, in thought controlled as much as possible by the influence of the unconscious) they have at once discovered a new Pierian spring, and rediscovered therein the old, and that through this discovery they have approached a goal such as the world never saw before. We are, as Freud has said, masses of unconsciousness no more than faintly illumined on the surface by the light of day; and this was said before Freud by the poets: Lautréamont, Rimbaud, Mallarmé, not forgetting Baudelaire. At the present stage of its development, poetry is in possession of a number of ways of attaining to the *symbol* – which, no longer controlled by the intellect, rises up by itself, redoubtable and wholly real. It is like a substance discharging force. And as the sensibility becomes accustomed, through training, to proceed from the phrase to the line of verse and from the commonplace word to the magic word, the quest for formal adequacy becomes inseparable from the quest for buried treasure. So may Poetry continue to advance '*dans l'absurde*', as they say!

This whole marvellous edifice is being shaken, as it happens, by another movement which we have begun to understand as being of unconscious origin and which is called Catastrophe. It would appear that the human soul is undergoing a fundamental upheaval, which may be destined to alter all appearances, to destroy both good and evil, and perhaps to make an end of man even while showing him the truth. At this very hour, civilization is faced with the possibility of the direst of catastrophes; a catastrophe all the more menacing in that its first and last cause lies within man's own inner depths, mysterious in their action and governed by an independent logic; moreover, man is now as never before aware of the pulse of Death within him. The psychoneurosis of the world has reached so advanced a stage that we can but fear the possibility of the act of suicide. Human society is reminded of the condition in which it found itself in the time of St John, or round about the year 1000; it awaits the end, hoping it will come soon. It should hardly be necessary to prove that the creator of living values (the poet) must be against catastrophe; the use the poet makes of the death-instinct is so entirely the contrary of that which catastrophe would make of it; and in a sense, poetry is the very life of the great Eros, surviving death *through* death. I have no faith in such poetry as chooses, by reason of unconscious processes, to continue embracing the corpse; the corpse can bring about no action, no revolution. God is life; and if finally death should have to become integrated with the world or with God, may such a thing never occur through the 'sense of the corpse' which man from the moment of his birth – such is the extraordinary fact – carries about with him wherever he goes, and which acts in him as a diabolical power engendering sin and guilt. And yet, for all we know, this diabolical power and the guilt which it involves may constitute the principal factors of human emancipation. Be that as it may, we find ourselves to-day heavy laden with the accumulated weight of instruments of Destruction; the noisome iniquities of its nations make of Europe 'the great harlot . . . seated upon a scarlet coloured beast, full of names of blasphemy, having seven heads and ten horns . . .' 'Alas, alas, that great city, that was clothed in fine linen, and purple, and scarlet, and decked with gold, and precious stones, and pearls! For in one hour so great riches is brought to nought.' We sense distinctly that it is a question not so much of imminent revolution as of sheer destruction, cultivation of a culpable object for our hatred, and regression.

Revolution, like the religious act, has need of love. Poetry is an inward vehicle of this love. We who are poets, therefore, must labour to bring forth, out of such base or precious substances as are derived from man's humble, beautiful erotic force, the *'bloody sweat'* of sublimation.

March 1933
(Avant-Propos to *Sueur de Sang*, Editions des Cahiers Libres, Paris, 1933)

Pierre Jean Jouve

THE PRESENT GREATNESS OF MOZART

Translated by David Gascoyne

It takes time for genius to become what it really is. Talent alone does
not seem to have to undergo the same time-process before it can
become apparent. Genius is at first like a tree that is too vast for
human sight, and not only is it possible for it to remain for a long time
unseen in its entirety, but also it may be seen in a distorting light and,
on account of the way the proportions of genius alter with time, will
make its appearance only gradually, by means of a slow discarding of
the qualities falsely attributed to it in the beginning. It can even change
in varying aspects within itself in order to correspond to new devel-
opments in human society; and it can and should be illumined by the
whole of human experience posterior to its historical appearance:
thus it becomes no longer the work of Mozart, but the work of the
universe. By that time we can no longer interpret the work of a genius
according to the explicit intentions of its creator or his opinions about
it: for we must realise that he whose spirit is truly profound is never
entirely conscious of his own creation; rather does his work impose
itself upon him and surpass him from the very start.

It has taken Shakespeare three centuries to reach something like
his true stature. Mediaeval French sculpture is now seen to constitute
the summit of occidental religious art. But Palestrina has scarcely
been perceived as yet. Real and artificial clouds still surround the
greatness of El Greco and of Poussin. Among all the varieties of
genius, the Genius of Music is that which has the greatest power of
motion, which has the most marvellous possibilities of transforma-
tion, is richest in purifying virtues, and propounds with greatest
difficulty the riddle of evolution through interpretation.

One hundred and fifty years have passed since Mozart first set out
in pursuit of his fulfilment, in order to stand at last revealed as it was

God's will he should be: as an absolute source of Music. He has had to pass through extraordinary disguises before reaching this apotheosis. The name of Wolfgang Amadeus Mozart has ever been a glorious one. But it is as though the first glory to be associated with him, the glory of the *prodigy*, had marked him with its inferior quality and relegated him to an epoch of brilliant worldliness, so that Mozart has been unable to escape from the misfortune of *success*. Behind the whole life, work and death of Mozart there is a significance the very opposite of that which has been attributed to them by that favourable tide which has swelled around him since the earliest days of his career; nevertheless this tide has carried him away with it. He was not lacking in admirers during the nineteenth century: Goethe declared that Mozart's music surpassed all, Delacroix adored him, Stendhal swore by 'Don Juan' alone; the 'divine' Mozart in fact was everywhere supreme; a 'Mozartian' air spelt invincible enchantment. It is legitimate to suppose that the adulations of such different types of mind were in accord only through misunderstanding. One has this suspicion, for example, when one compares Delacroix's opinion, in his Journal, of Mozart, with his opinion of the last works of Beethoven. What Delacroix liked about Mozart was not at all what he *ought* to have liked, being Delacroix, and being so powerfully attracted by Faust and Hamlet. No – at that time Mozart *was not yet visible*. Instead, there was universally recognised a figure based on all the Mozartian virtues – lightness, grace, tenderness, vivacity and proportion – a figure that became entirely substituted for the true Mozart. The kind of interpretation which gives chief importance to lightness, tenderness and grace, progressively strengthened the image of a delightful and seductive figure, and strengthened it moreover with values borrowed from the scale of truth, but ultimately untrue because of the accent placed upon them.

This labour of deception caused Mozart to withdraw into the realm of shadows. When the Wagnerian invasion set out to conquer Music, he almost disappeared. At the time of our youth (this was in France) Mozart, it seems to me now, was as remote as Rameau and as eighteenth-century as Glück. He was quite a small figure, a charming little marquis in a perruque and silken knee-breeches, tuning the violin upon his knee. Mozart became the synonym of all that is innocent and childlike in music, deliberately unconscious of all the wretchedness of life and completely unrelated to it; he became as affected and successfully executed as a sentimental Watteau – the pretty Mozart.

*

'Not a day passes but that I think of death', wrote Mozart at the most successful moment of his youth. 'Only from time to time I suffer from as it were fits of melancholy,' says another letter, written to his father in 1778. And then there is that extraordinary letter belonging to the final period, concerning the *Requiem:* 'I am about to breathe my last. I have reached the end before having fully enjoyed my talent. Yet life has been so beautiful and my career was opening under such fortunate auspices! . . . But one cannot change one's destiny. No man can number his days; one must be resigned; the will of Providence will be accomplished. I am making an end, this is my funeral chant and I must not leave it unperfected.'

*

It is perfectly certain that Mozart's genius is situated beneath the sign of death. Death presides over the origin of a marvellously perfect form, of a 'limit' exquisitely touched and always fulfilled exactly – right to the end. But this is still too general. The pure operation of the spirits of life and death in Mozart consists in a domination (perhaps unique) of the spirit of reason, illumined by Faith, and conforming to the golden rule of beauty, over the most violent forces of concupiscence, grief, melancholy, mockery and fury – demoniac and obsessional – over the cruellest realities that exist in fact – over sin itself. The part played by death in the work of Mozart is entirely spiritual: in it, death is the sister of fire. The enigma is centred around beauty: that this beauty should be constant, and that it should always reveal the inner suffering beneath.

In a certain sense, there is something inhuman (or superhuman) in Mozart's work. Probably it is that there is something miraculous for us in what he has to say. Mozart does indeed perform a miracle; and it is hardly surprising that it is difficult for most men to hear it. As Bruno Walter has so well said, the false Mozart was invented by those superficial people who, deaf to the things of the spirit, turned Mozart's virtues against Mozart himself; who made of the power of light a glittering adornment, and rendered invisible the secret grief. Mozart has been laid open to censure by his own admirers; for too long has admiration stood between his work and its true understanding. The lucidity and painful conflict of our own epoch was necessary before Mozart could reappear – in the guise, this time, of an archangel.

Mozart cannot be explained by his own utterances. What he himself said about his work has very little importance. This strange and fantastically proportioned genius keeps his work in dependence on that quality of the bizarre which distinguishes his own person; he is anti-Goethian in the sense that he knows nothing whatever about himself and *has* to continue in this blessed ignorance. He is conscious simply of having to be entirely song, entirely music; of being able (as one of his letters from Italy proudly announces) to compose in every style. It was surely a paradox of genius that caused Mozart to go to Italy in order to learn there to be *only* Mozart, to create a style inimitable from the first note on, and to produce with the aid of superficial Italy what Italy herself could never have produced, the Mozart world.

Yet 'in every style' does not truly represent the scope of his work, from *Idomeneo* to the *Requiem*. Forty-one symphonies (three of which are outstandingly great), all the works of chamber music and the concertos, twenty-four ballet-operas and six operas, sixteen masses and a quantity of pieces of religious music for choir – 620 works in all, and Mozart died at the age of thirty-five. He certainly is a prodigy – in this case in the plane of creation. But I am trying to distinguish another characteristic of his greatness. There are certain mysteries of sound which are too lofty, too complex, and too sacred to be caught by words. But we can say, nevertheless, that when we now hear, conducted by Bruno Walter, the principal symphonies or *Don Giovanni*, when we receive the grace of the *Qui tollis* from the *Great Mass in C minor*, or of the *Kyrie* from the *Requiem*, when our heart is searched by the *Ave verum corpus*, if we look for a standard by which to measure the force of our emotions, if we wish to find a symbol of 'equivalent greatness' in poetry, we can think only of Shakespeare – and even then Mozart's religious side has to be left singularly unaccounted for. (Of course such comparisons are basically false: what aspect of Shakespeare is in question? None of his aspects but rather a certain spirit of visionary solemnity, a tone of 'sovereign loftiness', and a tragic extremism resolved by beauty; in short, the essential Shakespearian quality itself.)

*

Of Mozart's polyphony it might be said that it has the substance of steel. Something extremely hard, yet as pliable as though it were perfectly soft. (Thus Don Juan, at the end of the first act, bends his sword against his breast, while singing against the chorus of lamentation, fury and remorse.) The violins play the leading rôle in this steel structure, which is formed by the opposition, the marriage, the marriage-conflict, between the wood-wind and the strings. But whether they are sad, or cruel, or smiling, these are the explosions of *hard* substances; the point cannot be too much stressed. In an extremely complex texture, difficult to grasp in its entirety, apparently simple in a cleverly deceptive way on account of its always being held together by the simple continuity of beauty, occur movements of dazzling strength, incessantly, while at the same time a series of marvellous developments, pursued to their furthest limits, separate them. *Rupture* is the law of this supreme harmonic art. What caused the appearance of music so essentially Music? The struggle of the soul against the soul, and of affect against affect, the heart-rending division, the wound – conflicting unity becoming divine unity. This unity is brought about only by renewing the incessant rupture. Mozart had to escape from his life in order to find his life. He performed this feat without an ounce of heaviness, with 'diabolical' lightness, and with all the central flame he could command. It should not be supposed that the Mozartian idea was always that of catharsis, or of ascent towards the light as in *The Magic Flute*. No, there is far more variety, human truth, despair, and error in Mozart's divine outpourings, a strong analogy with the pitiless onward movement of Shakespeare. As musician and as dramatist, Mozart has a complete mastery both of variety and of truth. 'Balance . . . truth' (Letter of 1782). There was nothing that could not be grasped by his mind so long as it adopted the *form* of his mind. His work is baroque and also Greek; both classical and modern; the least that can be said of it is that it represents something never to be found in the works of others. In the rapid unfolding of this savage and exquisite music, the greatest amount of force in every register of the orchestra and of the voice is brought into play, in order to reunite several varieties of genius: genius of invention, genius of proportion, and genius of childhood.

*

It has not been written with sufficient emphasis that of all mystical composers Mozart is closest to us, and that, by means of the art of sounds, he has manifestly easy access to the mystical life, and that the essentially Christian mystical being in Mozart is not absolutely confined to religious expression according to the Catholic faith. Mozart belongs to a time when all the modes of modern thought, the reign of Catholicism still being absolute, were able to find a place within Catholicism and when the liberty of the religious concept was only just beginning to grow. Mozart's religious temperament was of too deep a nature to be able to find full expression in the facile Catholic habits of his life. But for him, as for all mystics, Christ is *real*, complete, unattainable and ineffable. When Mozart writes on the theme of Christ (the solo *et incarnatus est* in the *Great Mass*, the motet *Ave verum corpus*) his song is of Christ, and of our humanity no longer. It is not that he is carried to his own summit like Bach, the summit of Moses on Sinai. He simply vanishes into ecstasy. What is still more surprising is that this disappearance takes place, I feel, within the very *spirit* of Mozart, at the moment when his mystical genius is at the height of its power. If we could study this situation very deeply, with the aid of instruments of psychic analysis such as we lack at present, we should perhaps find an explanation of the possible relation between mysticism, negation of art, and that form of art which is most highly developed from the artistic point of view.

One cannot neglect to consider the phenomenal scope of Mozart's work, and, within this work, the scope of the religious side of it. When in 1791 Mozart wrote, in a letter to the Municipality of Vienna soliciting a chapel-master's post, 'My wide knowledge of the religious style encourages me to believe myself more capable than others might be,' he was stating the truth, and it is to be remarked that he credited existence to a religious style of which he is the inheritor and continuer. But this question leads one to consider a situation much more general in ancient art, particularly in music, a doctrinal situation uniting creation to tradition, by means of singularly efficacious ties. There is no doubt that in its monumental, rigidly contrapuntal passages, Mozart's style is indeed indebted to certain predecessors, Italian and German chapel-masters and no doubt to Handel (particularly in the *Kyrie* of the *Requiem,* which is at the same time one of the peaks of the 'monumental' side of Mozart's work). But at the age of seventeen Mozart wrote at Milan a motet *Exsultate,* the inventiveness, the aerial mysteriousness and jubilant spirit of which are entirely personal to him; and it was really then that Mozart's religious style was created, a style uniting – as it is particularly interesting to note – both archaic and severe, and tender and human elements, and accomplishing this by completely 'burning' that grace which is profane in the sacred fire.

But the scope of Mozart's more untrammelled thought is almost inconceivable, ranging as it does from concertos to masses, from symphonies to motets, from tender to tragic operas, from quartets to serenades. The composition of the motet *Ave verum* belongs to the time when Mozart was working on the *Zauberflöte.* His religious and almost irreligious genius (does not *The Magic Flute* betray the subterranean influence of the French Revolution with its cult of Reason?) escapes from all ideal categories and, like that of Shakespeare, is at one and the same time atheistic, believing, spiritual and magical. We have no longer a scale by which to measure the size of such men. Our beings have become too small and the social troubles that weigh us down too great.

I see in Mozart the most modern of the old musicians. Because of his suffering and his hardness and his tendency towards the superhuman, he represents all that is craved for by the best in us, by that part of ourselves that has been least worn away. He represents it more clearly than any other master of music, except Bach. An opera like *Fidelio* (the most Beethovenian of all Beethoven's works) uplifts us with its irrepressible burning force, with the breath of that quality for which the German name is *Die Treue*. When destiny is unrolled (in the *Leonora* overture No.3 executed to perfection by Toscanini) in all its infinite dimension – such destiny as man is yet capable of *bearing* – it is really with man's past that we are confronted, and a shower of inward tears accompanies our nostalgia. Yet Mozart, having passed through this world previously, still finds himself beyond. He keeps the faith no longer, but helps us intermittently to evade our responsibility. Beethoven revives within us our deep feeling of responsibility in order that faith may triumph over sin. Mozart tears us away from it, wishing us to be *elsewhere*. The 'little fellow' of the letters to Constance Mozart has the power to do this, he has it to a divine degree. And to break with this world, by making beauty intervene in it, is undoubtedly the task with which we moderns are faced today.

*

Mozart's aversion to Salzburg, his birth-place, was very strong and persistent. 'You know ... how odious Salzburg is to me. Everywhere else I have much greater hope of being able to live satisfied and happy ... You now have the opinion of a true *patriot*.' (Letter from Paris 1778.)

As one walked through beautiful Salzburg, Salzburg of the Medicis, Italian town metamorphosized, grave, homely and aerial, but with also its nightmare aspect, the salt-mines, the catacombs in the enormous rocky walls; a town that might have been *found* in the work of Piranesi; as one walked through Salzburg, one could not help being struck by the identity which existed somehow between the genius of the town and the genius of Mozart. What does this mean? Mozart hated what he most certainly had loved and which united him by blood with the earth. I scrutinise the powerful and moulded but violently anxious face in Lange's portrait. Its feminine character makes one feel astonished and a little uneasy. The drama between oneself and one's country, another form of the drama between oneself and the mother, oneself and birth, suddenly appeared to me as though inscribed within the heavy matter of those eyes. And yet the face as a whole is like an illuminating globe – *like a sun.* Does not that seem to suggest that the painful and bitter cleavage from the material force, which he later reabsorbed, as it were, was redeemed by his marrying the sun? Redemption of the mother by the father, election by Jupiter, the initiation in *The Magic Flute,* such would appear to be Mozart's destiny. The puerile aspect of his sentimental life, the irresponsible aspect of his actions, also the sombre aspect of the time when the angel was gradually dying in him, the precocity and the haste of genius, the very brevity of his existence, are to be explained only by referring to the highest form of tragedy. *Don Giovanni,* situated at the cross-roads, takes on proportions of truly grandiose significance. Mozart was sent to the earth in order not to love, not to accept, not to endure, and yet to love, to be overflowing with love by these very means. Mozart died a child. Nothing of the wonder of the child was ever extinguished in him – before death. When he died in this marvellous fashion (as though his childhood was augmented towards the end, the *Zauberflöte* being the most childlike of all his works) Mozart accomplished a destiny the like of which has never been seen on earth again.

Grandeur actuelle de Mozart (1937)
[First published in *Horizon,* Vol. 1, No. 2 (February 1940)]

Bernard Groethuysen

CONCERNING THE POEMS OF HÖLDERLIN'S MADNESS

Translated by David Gascoyne

They were three friends who had met in the old monastery of the Augustinians, at Tübingen, when pursuing their classical studies: Hegel, Hölderlin and Schelling. The same love of antiquity and the same philosophical faith united all three of them. They studied Plato, Kant and Jacobi's letters on Spinoza.

So reading and discussing together everything from ancient times until the French Revolution, they had formed a vision of the universe and had no doubt that they would find again, whatever the encounters that life held in store for them, the unity and deep underlying meaning of things.

The three friends, on leaving the seminary at Tübingen, found themselves feeling much out of their element in the world outside. They didn't understand the language of the country, and the inhabitants understood them with difficulty. 'That which is without words, for him becomes word; that which is general and resides in the form of the unconscious, for him takes the form of the conscious and of the concrete; on the other hand, that which can be translated into words is for him that which couldn't be said or that ought not to be expressed; that which is concrete and conscious becomes for him unconscious and abstract,' says Hölderlin, speaking of the hero of his tragedy: Empedocles.

The three friends easily understood the language of Empedocles, but they could scarcely find agreement with the bourgeois people among whom they were going to become tutors. 'When occasionally I chance to speak with a certain degree of warmth about ancient Greece, they yawn and answer me that, after all, one must also live in the present time,' says Hyperion speaking of the bourgeois of Smyrna.

Hegel and Schelling nevertheless got to know, in time, how to force their views on the 'bourgeoisie'. As philosophers, they made their way forward to protect their world from the arguments which for some time had been troubling people's minds. Hölderlin, who had remained a poet, attempted nothing of that kind. More timid than his friends, and having nothing about him of an intellectual conqueror, he knew neither how to make others adopt the language he spoke himself nor how to learn theirs.

> *I understand the great silence of the Aether,*
> *The word of man I never understood.*

So he had no proofs to demonstrate the existence of the world in which he lived. This world was divine, and because it was divine it was without God. For if every thing is divine, there is no God, there are only the gods. The divine has no name; only the gods have, whose number is not precisely fixed and who from time to time change form.

Existence is divine; to be what one is, is to be divine. Plants are divine, and the stars are divine, and the Aether, which is an image of the divinity. All is there, simple in itself, and knowing no other end than to be forever; and the seasons which follow one after another, and the hours of the day in their unvarying rhythm reveal to us that the Whole is perfect, that everything is divine.

Everything that is therefore asks nothing more than to be. Only man, not recognizing his own limits, does not know where to settle in a world where everything is at rest. The plant calls to him, and reveals to him the life which, unaware of itself, blends into the great whole. But he, not hearing the divine rhythm by which everything is controlled, is nowhere at home, and anxiety unceasingly pursues him.

Sometimes however, the gods who dwell in a serene light and know nothing of the anxious cares of the half-light below, happen to start loving him, and even to seek his love in return, for the nostalgia for the divine which is the distinctive characteristic of man, reflects back to them their own image projected into the infinite, and the anxieties of those who love them awaken in them the feeling of their own happiness.

But among these gods who 'dwell up there in the light' and do not know of any fate, where is he, he who knows how to speak to man of his sufferings? Where is the Christ, brother of Hercules and Dionysus, the last of the ancient gods? He has come at a late hour, into a divine world; the human soul nevertheless had been seeking for him for a long while; for he understands it, when amid the silence of all surrounding things it listens and asks questions of itself. However, after a moment of surrender, it withdraws, and timidly conceals itself, afraid of not knowing any longer how to love sufficiently the stars and flowers, and of breaking the silence which hovers over the whole.

But Dionysus has rejoined his brother, Christ, who has survived God. God is dead, and the world is alone. Everything has a silent beauty which reminds us of the absent one. Everything is at rest and slowly flows away.

Yet the soul remains anxious. It calls upon its God, it feels itself imprisoned. Before it lies the Infinite. The Infinite and the finite; it seems to Hölderlin that all his anguish has its only origin in the conflict which now divides them. There is the tranquil and consistent life of those who, having recognised their limits, have found their proper home. 'Why cannot I be like them,' Hölderlin asks himself. 'I could be a pastor in one of these little Württemberg villages and the days would follow one another in a life filled with long hours, smooth and united. And is not the Infinite in the finite? In a much limited existence, man can also live an infinite life, and his Divinity which is but the God of this life will be infinite.'

His mother writes to him: 'Come to live with us, you will be better here.' He replies: 'I will come, and you will be with me.' But he cannot. 'Empedocles, hostile to everything that might determine his life in any one or another way, and as a result dissatisfied, even though that which surrounds him does not lack beauty, anxious, full of anguish as soon as he has to give himself up to a particular way of life - for he can only conceive of life as being in his union with all life – being unable to live like a god, extend his heart without limit to everything which lives, and love with a total love – for the Whole presents itself to him only under the form of successive impressions,' Empedocles will never be able to find rest.

He must have the Whole, he wouldn't know how to live elsewhere. There's nothing which does not remind him of this; he cannot be unfaithful to it for it is the beauty of the Whole which gives all things their beauty, and makes us conceive the idea that everything is divine. Wherever I go, I must find the beautiful again, he had told himself. The world has absorbed God: how could all things not be beautiful? That's what he had believed before knowing the world, and he continued to believe it when he acquired knowledge of people and places, seeking everywhere and always for the vision of the Whole, which is before all things. One must know how to see the Whole before its parts, and nothing must be placed apart or set in isolation. Only thus can all things be beautiful, when everything in the distance melts together, and becomes one: a world. For nothing can be beautiful separately, the total beauty must be found in everything, beauty in its integrity.

Hölderlin complains in one of his letters that he can only see things on a grand scale and as though bathed in light, and that his poetry is lacking in nuances and shades. In each of his poems, one might say that he makes one enter a world; his work is the universe in which he lives.

'What are you searching for?' Diotima asks Hyperion. 'It's not for something that may have disappeared, many years ago, – one can't exactly say when whatever it was was and when it was not. But it was once, and it is still, it is in yourself,' she says. Now it is precisely not being able to find it in himself that is the cause of his great suffering. 'You wanted a world,' Diotima tells him, 'that's why you have everything, and you have nothing.'

There was a moment in his life when he believed he had found this world and that he could love it as one loves a being who is very close to you and who listens to you. The Whole is beautiful. Can the poet come across in the being he loves what he was able to find again only in himself?

Then, no more solitude. The world is there. It has taken form. It has come to the poet. The poet takes it and embraces it. You are mine. From henceforth nothing can separate us. My soul has gone out to meet with yours. In listening to your voice, I shall no longer know the anguished states of old. The Infinite is you, the Infinite in the finite. I no longer search for it elsewhere; I will go no more in search of it far away.

The I has found the Thou the poet had vainly invoked in the silence of the Whole. A voice has answered to his love. From now on the soul will no longer be alone.

And that was his great mistake. The voice has become silent, and the poet has experienced the fears of the solitude which knows itself for what it is, and of the silence which listens to itself alone. Then he discovers a new world, the world of the traveller who sees everything for the first time. It is no longer his soul that can interpret this new world for him, and he begins to listen to voices, which come to him from without. He travels, and experiences strange things such as are scarcely to be understood and which are difficult to express. One must know how to keep silent, and not let one's own voice get confused with all this. But how to find yourself again in this world which is no longer yours and in which man could not dwell? The traveller tries to embrace its contours, and the lands he travels through are drawn as though upon a map of the world.

So Hölderlin's soul went travelling. And from its travels it brought back great splendours and deep anguishes. It went far away and lived in various times, among the gods and among men. It took note of what it saw and was possessed of the great desire to say nothing that was not true. Formerly, the poet had thought the soul sufficed to render what he had seen; but now the soul knows that the world is there, and that one must listen for a long while, and that in the great silence of ourselves it is scarcely granted us to render the voices that come to us from every side and the images that pass by when one flies over the lands below. But sometimes the sounds and the images escape him and become confused, or rather it does not know how to render them exactly as they were and without mixing something of its own with them. It is in these moments that it feels a deep distress because it is afraid of losing the images and no longer hearing the sounds from the moment it is no longer sure of being able to fix them.

Therefore it goes on long voyages and tries to say what it sees; but never did it find itself so alone. For those who stay at home remain in themselves, and a great solitude unites all men. But those who travel far and hear voices unheard by the others, do not know community. They know that they are not understood. Nor at the same time can they keep silence; for one must speak of what one has seen. The voices demand it and one cannot disobey them.

There is no way of getting out of this situation. But the voices become silent after a time. Or else is it that you no longer resist them and that they no longer demand that you should speak? If they question you, you will make verses for them. They pass and go away. That is not greatly important. They are from that other world, and they are well established there. One must leave them where they are. But you? You are wise, with a deep wisdom, wise as are only madmen and children. A child knows many things, but he doesn't know them in our way. He travels a lot, but not in the way we travel. Besides, how could he talk to grown-ups who understand so badly what one says to them?

But it is a child who remembers; a child remembers that he has been one of these adults who now come to see him and regard him with curiosity. He speaks to them of the years that pass by, of the seasons that return, of the morning hour in spring, of harvest days, of the Sundays when one relaxes, of the churchyard where man and woman sleep. For he knows all that, and many other things as well. But he knows them in a way that is different from that in which those who question him know them; more simply, one might say, and with fewer words. The others know them by means of well-linked sentences, and they are very satisfied with them, for that is for them a way of situating things and building-up wholes. He sometimes stops abruptly and falls silent. That's because the others cannot understand.

For they want everything to be completed in a well-ordered series. But he after a long silence takes up his thought again. He knows that not everything is to be said or explained, and that in any case it is not necessary to speak.

One must not try to make them all agree. What would be the use? Yet they have all been children. But it is hardly given to everyone to know what we all knew when we were children, and at the same time to possess the deep wisdom of those who have finished with living.

NOTE: 'This text first appeared as Preface (*Avant-Propos*) to the translations made in collaboration by Pierre Jean Jouve and Pierre Klossowski (brother of the painter Balthus) of a selection of the poems written by Hölderlin after the onset of his madness (approx. 1802); first published in 1930 under the title *Poèmes de la Folie de Hölderlin*; new edition published by Gallimard in 1963.' D. G.

APPENDIX A

A1 'The ascetic sensualist'

A2 'My Indebtedness to Jouve'

A3 Drafts of 'Mozart: Sursum Corda'

A4 'Elegiac Stanzas In Memory of Alban Berg' (unpublished)

A5 *Strophes Elégiaques à la mémoire d'Alban Berg*

A6 Two early Jouve translations by David Gascoyne

A7 Draft of 'Post Mortem' (unpublished)

A8 Two letters from David Gascoyne to *Poetry* (London)

A9 'Yes, You!' and Untitled (unpublished)

A10 Two letters from Pierre Jean Jouve to David Gascoyne

A11 Two letters from Blanche Reverchon-Jouve to David Gascoyne

A12 'A New Poem by Pierre Jean Jouve: "Language"'

David Gascoyne

PIERRE JEAN JOUVE
The ascetic sensualist [33]

When Pierre Jean Jouve died in 1976, at the age of ninety-one, he left behind him two distinct bodies of writing, the first of which he had come to regard as 'manqué' and unworthy of perpetuation. In 1925, as the result of a spiritual crisis, a radical change of direction and remarriage, he rejected *en bloc* as unsatisfactory some twenty items published during nearly twenty years. Three years later, in the 'post-face' to *Noces*, the first collection Jouve considered authentically representative, he declared: 'The poetic principle obliges the poet to disown his first work.'

The decisive factor determining the *vita nuova* Jouve was to undertake after the end of the First World War was his relationship with Blanche Reverchon, a friend of his wife nine years his senior who, when he first met her in Florence, and then in Salzburg, during the course of 1921, was already a practising doctor and psychiatrist. Their subsequent marriage in 1925 resulted in fifty years of fruitful companionship. Jouve's inner life, influenced by mystics such as Ruysbroeck, Teresa of Avila and John of the Cross, and to be found reflected in the poems of *Noces*, was soon to become, through association with his second wife an inner life conceived as grounded in the Unconscious, site of the Eros / Thanatos conflict and of *la scène capitale*. In 1960, Jouve published a sequence called simply *Proses*, which contains the poem 'Trésor', the subject of which is unmistakable:

> *Tu es trésor par l'intervention que tu as osé faire jadis pour transformer en moi cent choses de profondeur, et me conduire à moi-*

---

33 Review of Pierre Jean Jouve, *Oeuvre*, Tome 1 et Tome II (Paris: Mercure de France, 1988). *Times Literary Supplement* (6 May 1988), p. 505.

même. Tu es trésor par la présence constante et fidèle à tous les tour-
billons, crises, malheurs passagers. . . .

The edition of his writings now published in celebration of the cente-
nary of Jouve's birth is aptly entitled *Oeuvre*: its two volumes, one
devoted to his poetry, the other to his prose, make their inter-
dependence more apparent than it may have been before. Its most
distinguishing feature, however, is that it unites for the first time
between the same covers the works rejected by their author in the
mid-1920s, and those issued between 1925 and the end of his life. In
each case the early work occupies the second half of the volume.
Much of it was published in slim and limited editions which, by the
1980s, had become extremely rare and difficult to obtain. In a brief
note prefacing Tome 1 of the *Oeuvre*, Yves Bonnefoy discusses 'Le prob-
lème des premiers livres' and persuasively argues the case for making
the suppressed work available to the increasing number of admirers
and students of Jouve. He regards it as not unworthy of the greater
author Jouve was later to become, and its republication as justifiable
above all by its revelation of the developing mastery of prosody which
distinguished Jouve's contribution to the poetry of his time.

The second half of the first volume of the present *Oeuvre* also
contains 100 pages of 'Textes retranchés', that is to say of poems and
stanzas from later, published collections that some compunction had
led the poet subsequently to discard. Immediately after restoring
these *disjecta membra*, the book turns back to reproduce in its entirety
Jouve's first *plaquette*, *Artificiel*, all but two copies of which appear
to have been destroyed soon after its appearance in 1909. Its first
pages reveal at least three constants: epigraphical quotations from
Mallarmé, whose influence was to become apparent again after 1945; a
dedication to Debussy, indicating an unusually strong empathy with
the art of music that remained Jouve's for life; and the presence in
the first line of the initial poem of the word *chevelure*, destined to play
a paramount role in the masterly novella of 1932, *Dans les années
profondes*, and in many of the 'Hélène' poems associated with it.

The publishers claim the Édition du Centenaire to be both exemplary and definitive, 'car jamais on n'était allé aussi loin dans la divulgation de l'oeuvre "interdite" d'un des plus grands écrivains de ce siècle.' If Jouve is indeed one of the greatest French writers of the century, then a fundamental reason for this is without doubt the uncompromising ruthlessness of his quest for perfection, the severity of his self-criticism. Having once achieved an assured notion of what constituted his mature aims as a writer, he pursued them with undeviating consistency. No one who knew Jouve during the period between the 1930s and '60s would be likely to forget his reluctance to discuss in any detail the work referred to here as *interdite*. If this later attitude, as expressed with laconic lucidity in certain passages of his autobiographical *En Miroir* (1954), can be described by Bonnefoy as resulting from a 'tension un peu trop délibérément hautaine', it was none the less wholly typical, for better or worse, of the artistic persona that Jouve had by then patiently evolved. Though the *Oeuvre* presented here – both its contents and the order of them – apparently accords with wishes expressed by Jouve before he died, it seems sadly ironic that so intransigent an artistic conscience should have ended by endorsing an – in some ways – unsatisfactory compromise.

Adequately to sum up here the principal characteristics of Jouve's post-1925 output would be impossible. Among eleven collections, the second, *Sueur de sang* (1933) together with its two pre-war sequels, is perhaps most representative and distinctive. It is prefaced by the essay, 'Inconscient, spiritualité et catastrophe', which amounts to a manifesto announcing the kind of poetry that had emerged from a full awareness of the unconscious mind as conceived by Freud, and of its relation to both the basest and the most sublime levels of the human psyche. The opening couplet of *Sueur de sang* sheds light both on this underlying dualism, and on the fascinating pair of novels Jouve was engaged in writing at about the same time:

> Les crachats sur l'asphalte m'ont toujours fait penser
> A la face imprimée au voile des saintes femmes.

The novels *Hécate* (1928) and *Vagadu* (1930), eventually reappeared in one volume entitled *Histoire de Catherine Crachat*. The heroine is a star of the silent screen, Garbo-cum-Lilian Harvey, who in the first part is seen reduced to a state of spiritual checkmate and moral aridity, but is gradually liberated, restored and transformed through psychoanalysis in the second part. The authenticity of this astonishing double narrative must be recognizable to anyone who has had the least experience of psychoanalysis. The technical skill of its presentation had already been evident in its two immediate predecessors. Precocious passion for an older married man, an equally ardent but thwarted religious vocation, murder of the beloved, years of imprisonment followed by self-banishment after release and a serene ultimate acceptance: these are the ingredients of a novel, *Paulina 1880* (1925), that should by now be recognized as a classic. It is set in nineteenth-century Italy, and is clearly inspired by Jouve's two years' residence in the neighbourhood of Florence. *Le Monde désert*, which followed it two years later, is equally remarkable but less easily summarized. Set in Switzerland at the end of the First World War, it is concerned with the troubled relationships uniting three characters: the homosexual son of a pastor, a French poet and a mysteriously fascinating Russian woman named Baladine (like the actual Mme Klossowska Jouve had known personally, friend of Rilke and mother of Pierre Klossowski and the painter Balthus). This triangular situation leads to a suicide which does not resolve the tension it entails but leaves it open towards the future.

Histoires sanglantes (1932) are described by Jean Starobinski in his introductory essay as a series of capriccios: tales of 'mystery and imagination' inspired by privileged familiarity with the catacombs opened by Freudian analysis, often subtly sardonic in tone. Their sequel, two *récits* entitled *La Scène capitale*, constitutes, as Starobinski says, 'sans doute le haut lieu de l'oeuvre narrative de Jouve'. In the final example of this narrative work, *Dans les années profondes*, Jouve succeeds in amalgamating in a single character of mythical proportions, Hélène de Sannis, elements drawn from a number of women who had played a role in his life. It is her *chevelure* that attracts the attention of the young Léonide when he first catches sight of her in a secret valley of the Engadine where he is on holiday. As soon as he has made her acquaintance, *la chevelure* becomes his obsession; 'Toujours plus belle, toujours plus mystérieuse, cette touffe, pleine de replis et de nuages, de reflets sanglants, de cavernes noires, dans laquelle mes regards se noyaient en éprouvant la volupté du plaisir de la mort.' The erotic adventure proceeding from this conjunction culminates in the death of Hélène in Léonide's arms at the climax of the sexual act. The theme of the interrelation between love and death that predominates throughout Jouve's writing never found better expression than here.

In 1946, Jouve opened a lecture (delivered in Oxford and London), 'L'Apologie du poète', by declaring: 'J'ai souvent pensé, tout au cours de ma vie, à une phrase d'Elizabeth Browning: "Le poéte est celui qui dit les choses essentielles".' Alongside this indication of his lifelong aspiration should be placed a previous avowal of the fundamental aim of his later poetry; 'Obtenir une langue de poésie qui se justifiat entièrement comme chant: et trouver dans l'acte poétique une perspective religieuse – seul réponse au néant du temps.' Though brought up a Catholic, Jouve escapes all easy categorization as a religious poet. He recognized in himself a residual puritanism, referred to by one of his critics as Jansenist. The 1938 preface to a new edition of his earlier *Paradis perdu* is entitled 'La Faute' and this text, significantly, employs the expression *Deus Absconditus*. Underpinning all his more specifically religious poetry is what has now long been known as 'negative theology', and in all that he wrote, as in his character, asceticism is inseparable from sensuality. The mystical and the erotic constantly alternate or merge in his work, as in that of Georges Bataille, though never in so equivocal a fashion. Jouve regarded the writer's task as 'la transformation incessante de la matière personnelle' and the alchemy of this process as summarised by the term 'sublimation'. His objectivization of his personal experience – both of the vicissitudes of sexuality and of the spirit's wrestling for faith – often took the form in his poetry of an approximation to musical composition. The poems consist largely of inventions, of suites and of variations on themes, and one of the forms of 'personal matter' transformed by Jouve in this way resulted from an exceptionally acute response to the power of music. A frequenter from their inception of the Salzburg festivals, an admirer and friend of Bruno Walter, Jouve found inspiration for poems above all in the works of Mozart and Alban Berg.

Both Jouve's full-length commentaries on operas (*Don Juan* and *Wozzeck*) are illustrated throughout by numerous quotations from the scores, and the second (*Wozzeck ou le nouvel opéra*) was written in collaboration with the musicologist Michel Fano. Both result from impassioned appreciation combined with a firm objective grasp of musical structure. Together they may well be considered an essential contribution to Jouve's total output; both are unfortunately excluded from the second volume of the *Oeuvre*, which in compensation makes available for the first time a suite of wholly uninhibited erotic notations dating from the 1930s, entitled *Les Beaux Masques*. This *inédit* is followed by a number of touchingly intimate fragments written after the death of Blanche in 1974.

The concluding 400 pages of Tome II are devoted to Jouve's work as a translator, and contain versions of work by a heterogeneous selection of poets: Tagore, Kipling, ('si curieusement brutal, religieux et fantaisiste à la fois'), Francis of Assisi, Hölderlin, Teresa of Avila, Góngora, Shakespeare (the Sonnets and 'The Phoenix and the Turtle') and even Montale and Ungaretti. A hypothetical further volume could reunite the translations of *Romeo and Juliet*, *Macbeth* and *Othello*, of Chekhov's *Three Sisters*, of Berg's reduction of Büchner's *Wozzeck* and of Wedekind's *Lulu* diptych.

One might consider that this edition of Jouve's *Oeuvre* is in some respects too complete, including material that might well have been reserved for a volume intended for specialists, and in others less complete than it might have been, had other priorities been preferred. Starobinski suggests that the present volumes should be followed by a third, which would contain not only the indispensable studies of

Don Juan and *Wozzeck,* but also Jouve's commentaries on Baudelaire, Delacroix, Meryon, Courbet, Balthus and Artaud, which contain writing as characteristic of him as anything to be found in his poetry or fiction. He also produced eloquent politico-historical texts concerning Danton and de Gaulle, and if the existing two volumes reveal Jouve as being more essentially European than the majority of his contemporaries, the latter grandiose texts, together with his exegeses of paintings by Delacroix and Courbet, represent an intense but idiosyncratic patriotism – also apparent in the many poems in which he celebrated such places as Larchant, les Saintes-Maries-de-la-Mer and Dieulefit. But it is impossible not to be grateful to Mercure de France and Jean Starobinski for having honoured this writer's centenary by making available nearly 4,000 pages of ever more rewarding writings. It undoubtedly fulfils the desire Jouve expressed in the concluding lines of his 1960 *Proses* (subtitled 'La voix, le sexe et la mort'):

> *Je ne veux de cloison avec l'oeuvre ni l'âme*
> *D'aucun son créateur au gouffre de mon temps.*

MY INDEBTEDNESS TO JOUVE [34]

Adam has asked me to write a few words about the importance of the music of Mozart. At his request I have translated four of Pierre Jean Jouve's poems that attest most clearly to the tremendous veneration that this great poet felt for Mozart's music during the later part of his life, particularly during the period shortly before the last war when these particular poems were written, and when Jouve was preparing his remarkable prose analysis of the opera *Don Juan*.

I am proud to have been the translator of the introductory essay to Jouve's book *Grandeur actuelle de Mozart* (which first appeared in the N.R.F.) and to have been able to persuade Cyril Connolly to publish it in English in an early issue of *Horizon*.[35] It was to this essay that I owe my first mature appreciation of the true significance and exceptional greatness of Mozart, as like so many supposedly musical people in the thirties, my idea of his music was very much the conventional one, in which the aspect of sunny charm and the pathos of prematurely carried-off genius combined to hide the profundity and sublimity that characterize the true Mozart.

I wish this note could be continued to the length of an essay of my own, though I have never had musicological pretensions and have none now, but happen to think that Michel Fano, Messiaen's pupil who collaborated with Jouve in writing two books of musically-technical and poetic analysis of Alban Berg's operas *Wozzeck* and *Lulu*, was right in believing that a music-loving poet can bring intuitive insights to the appreciation of a composer with whom he feels a special affinity, or to whom he is indebted, that are of more value than some of the stricter school of music critics would be likely to admit. But I know very well I could never hope to approach the quality of understanding and the beauty and aptness of language, that Pierre Jean Jouve achieved whenever he wrote about music.

34 First published in *Adam International Review*, 422/424 (1980), pp. 52–3.
35 *Horizon*, Vol. 1, No. 2 (February 1940), pp. 84–94. Gascoyne's translation was included in *Mozart's Don Juan* by Pierre Jean Jouve, translated from the French by Eric Earnshaw Smith (London: Vincent Stuart, 1952), pp. 1–10. The essay was reprinted in a limited edition (Birmingham: Delos Press 1996).

Mozart: 'Sursum Corda'
Draft in Notebook

Filters the sunlight from the knife-bright wound
And rarifies the { rumour
{ image-laden air
The { all-receptive heart in pure hands held
{ ~~elevated~~
Towards the sostenuto of the sky

{ Supernal voices, flood the ear of clay,
{ ~~Angelic~~
And { pierce through the dense skull! reveal
{ ~~break the crystal skull~~
The immaterial world concealed
By mortal deafness and the screen of sense:

World of transparency and utmost flight,
And world within the world: beyond our speech
To tell what equinoxes of { the absolute
{ ~~unclouded space~~
The spirit ranges in its long upwards release.

~~Filters the sunlight from the knife-bright wind~~
And catches all the colour of the air }
~~And rarifies the rumour-burdened air~~ }
~~The all-receptive chalice of the heart upheld~~
~~Towards the sostenuto of the sky~~

Filters the sunlight from the knife-bright wind
And rarifies the rumour-burdened air
The heart's receptive chalice in pure hands upheld
Towards the sostenuto of the sky.

World of transparency and last release,
And world within the world: beyond our speech
To tell what equinoxes of the infinite
The spirit ranges in its utmost flight.

Published Version
Seven, No. 4 Summer 1939, p. 33.
For Priaulx Renier [sic]

Filters the sunlight from the knife-bright wind
And rarifies the rumour-burdened air
The heart's receptive chalice in pure hands upheld
Towards the sostenuto of the sky

Supernal voices flood the ear of clay
And transpierce the dense skull: Reveal
The immaterial world concealed
By mortal deafness and the screen of sense,

World of transparency and last release
And world within the world! Beyond our speech
To tell what equinoxes of the infinite
The spirit ranges in its rare utmost flight.

Elegiac Stanzas in Memory of Alban Berg

First draft, British Library (Add. 56041, 56043)

I

When a rich (sick) rose falls in flakes from its thorn-spiked stem
Its petals stain the dark eroded soil;
So tears fall heavily to stain the heart's stone floor
A grief akin to madness sets its sudden springs
To leap without a cause from out our sleep
Our (jarring) nervous dreams
Until we shake with sorrow that we cannot name.

The rain with turbid drops adorns the leaves
Of rose-bushes that grow among the rocks
And stifle with their scent the chilly air.
It is the hour when disembodied heads,
The faces of the lost, glide, pensively
Across (Along / Among) the misty twilight (shadows) of this
            distant place, –
Cimmeria, the refuge of the shades.

On high
Striations of white light amaze the sky;
While round the staring lead-eyed pool below
A dull wind stirs the agony of reeds
Concentric ripples strike the water's rim
Like echoes of a desperate final cry,
And (While) arrow-headed birds fly fast away.

II

The snake-like roads that writhe across the plains
The agonized cities and towns

The valleys of melting snow
And the cruel mountain heights
By day lie exposed to the blows of the sun
Are oppressed under darkness by night
And have never repose

Or monotonous colourless skies
Weigh down the appalling /dreadful streets
Where human misery seems too great to bear –
Thugs trained to beat the poor to death
Neurotics groping in distress; –
Or fear-distended eyes through windows see
The glare of gasworks bursting on the outskirts of the town.
Lying tired and silent in a darkened room
One hears the trains rush by across the viaduct
Raucously hastening to attain the heart of Europe
And one lies wondering:
Where can all the trains be going?
Why is it all the trains are crashing
In my head?

III

[Dream, desire, death, all told,
The present's pain,
Centreless, all-pervading,
Drowns in its daft white glare
The dissolving world retracts
Its image from our eyes]

The world dissolves, retracts
Its image from the eye's
Dissolving glare. The present's pain
(Dream, desire, death all told)

Centreless, (ever-present) pervading all,
Drowns in its daft white glare
The mind as music drowns

Us, listening on the … verge
Of virgin silence, that last
Comfort of the battered, and it seems
Its sense is stronger than the eye's;
No words, no passionate description
Can move us more than these:
'*Les sons d'une musique enervante et calme.*

Semblable au cri lontain de l'humaine douleur,'
Too complicated to explain,
Too like a wound (cruelly true) to bear for long
Before the wind rises again at last.
Blowing the hair back from our heads,
And snatching away the music in our ears
To lose it in the vast sky's sombre waste

[*The stanza below is written on a separate page
under the heading* IV]

[A man's life now, like the wind
That passes, the winds above us,
No longer fixed nor separate in itself
But with all the others merging,
As where a lonely column melts
Into the distance and the breast of doves
Are seen a moment as they cross the brow.]

Elegiac Stanzas IV

As the wind strikes light from the sides
Of waves and silver from their crests
Though of no Southern Ocean but the couch
Of gloom and icebergs, as the wind
[That passes in its passing wrests
(A transitory smile) from (the) rock
Grinds one more grain of sand
From rock]
That passes in its passing wrests
A transitory smile from utter rock
And stirs the sleep of sand,
As where a single column melts
Into the distance and the wings (breasts) of doves
Whirl for a moment past the gazer's eyes,
As smoke climbs up behind a hill
To tell of towns or tents beyond,
And as these vaguer images
Merge one by one into a waking dream,

A man's life passes, is not fixed or one,
But is not substanceless as (things)
In all the loud apocalypse of time,
One man or millions, (each is set)
from which no-one escapes
The place and date. Man's present state
How fearful, and how real.

V

A sombre script in half-light read
Text of an ancient or some sage
Transfigured by a sudden inward ray
That floods the meditative page

Instructs the bewildered heart:
Death is not only death nor yet
Shall life prevail if death should die

Whose is the memory we mourn?
But countless memories, innumerable stones,
Each spark that the dark defeated
And at last shall kindle in a blinding
Blaze, make mourning seem
A child's misapprehending weakness, when
Flame leaps from the very urn.

An ancient text – but we do not look back
But forward out of meditation rear
A dustless and determined clear
Inscription like a fervent pointing hand:
We lived this time and saw
Ruin and death at work on every side –
We also saw your light who burn/shine ahead
(But never doubted)

*

Elegiac Stanzas in Memory of Alban Berg

Second draft, in the Berg Collection, New York Public Library

I

When a rich rose falls in flakes from a thorn-spiked stem
Its petals stain the dark eroded soil;
So tears fall heavily to stain the heart's stone floor.
A grief near madness sets its sudden springs
To leap without a cause from out our sleep,
Our jarring nervous dreams,

Until we shake with sorrow that we cannot name.
The rain with turbid drops adorns the leaves
Of rose-bushes that grow among the rocks
And stifle with their scent the chilly air.
It is the hour when disembodied heads,
The faces of the lost, glide pensively
Across the twilight of this distant place, –
Cimmeria, the refuge of the shades.

On high
Striations of white light amaze the sky;
While round the staring lead-eyed pool below
A dull wind stirs the agony of reeds,
Concentric ripples strike the water's rim
Like echoes of a desperate final cry;
And arrow-headed birds fly fast away.

II

The roads that writhe across the plains
The harrowed upland fields
The valleys of melting snow
And the cruel mountain heights
By day lie exposed to the blows of the sun
Are oppressed under darkness by night
And have never repose

Our monotonous colourless skies
Weigh down the appalling streets
Where human misery seems too great to bear:
Thugs trained to beat the poor to death
Neurotics gasping in distress
Or fear-distended eyes through windows see
The glare of gasworks bursting on the outskirts of the town.

Lying tired and silent in a darkened room
One hears the trains rush by across the viaduct
Raucously hastening to attain the heart of Europe;
And one lies wondering:
Where can all the trains be going?
Why is it all the trains are crashing
In my head?

Strophes Elégiaques
à la Mémoire d'Alban Berg (1885–1935)

The titles of the first, second and fourth parts of the following sequence were taken from Berg's 'Lyric Suite'. Lines 14 and 15 of the third part are a quotation from a poem in Baudelaire's sequence 'Le Vin', which was set to music by Berg as a cantata.

Two earlier versions of these Strophes were written in English, but were not satisfactory enough to be printed. The following version, written in 1939, three years after the original impulse, appeared in 'Cahiers du Sud' in January 1940.
D. G.

Andante Amoroso

Souvenir d'un musicien: des cordes lyriques
Soulèvent des draps de brume et l'ouïe est entrainée
Parmi des perspectives dissolvantes où son élégie
Fleurit comme une couronne qu'arrosent des pleurs
De sons: orchidées couleur d'ecchymose, et roses
Flétries, fleurs de la passion, une gerbe flottante
Lente à travers la vue des yeux fermés.

Sa musique est une pluie qui rafraîchit
Les cyprès seuls parmis ces rochers gris,
Trouble comme l'amour dans la mémoire les airs
Du soir, à l'heure où la hantise et l'obsession,
Figures du passé, glissent comme des têtes coupées
Sur les courants du crépuscule lointain
De Cimmérie, refuge des ombres perdues.

L'illusion tremble. En haut, aigües
Des lames de lumière crue incisent les cieux;
Et au-dessous, autour d'un lac de plomb
Le vent agite des roseaux dissonants;
Des vagues concentriques frappent le bord de l'eau

Comme les échos d'un cri désespéré.
Très vite s'envolent des oiseaux comme des flèches.

Tenebroso

Les grandes plaines où les routes sont comme des veines,
Les rangs de montagnes et les lacs réfléchissants,
Même les prairies les plus vides ou fleuries
Portent l'ombre énorme du *Zeitgeist,* qui menace
Avec ses nuages noirs de sort solides
Toutes les moissons; les saisons ne font plus
Qu'illustrer les phases des luttes humaines.

Et au-dessûs du chaos des grandes villes
Qui gonfle le continent, la noirceur des ceux pèse
Comme un jugement sur toutes les rues-prisons
Où rôdent encore les peurs de l'ancienne nuit
Avec des uniformes, des bâtons, des fusils,
Et où la folie couve ses fantaisies
De persécutés, d'espions, d'élus de Dieu.

Nous couchés sans sommeil dans nos chambres séparées
Nous écoutons un fracas comme de trains-fantômes
Se précipitant vers le bout de nos souffrances;
Et tandis que leur tonnerre ruine nos rêves on se demande
Quel grand minuit peut être le but de leurs roues chaudes,
Quel signe pourrait empêcher tout espoir comme un train fou
De se dérailler dans la tête de l'homme.

Intermezzo

Tout chant est triomphe et toute plainte
Est réconciliation. Brûle encore,
Brûle, O lyre du larynx, guérisse le tourment
Qui ne sait pas trouver une sortie
Parmi le labyrinthe de la poitrine. Encore

Plongez-vous dans la mélodie, O ailes sonores
A la recherche de repos et de paix.

Toute plainte est réconciliation
Avec le lamentable, et sait résoudre
Les pleurs et les ruines, la maladie
Des empires, dans des arabesques
De cancereuse corruption et de pluie
D'étincelante semence stérile, tels que
'Les sons d'une musique énervante et câline,

'Semblable au cri lointain de l'humaine douleur;'
Et une telle musique peut nous consoler
De la condition damnée, la blessure secrète,
Qui grimpant vers le silence à travers l'oreille
Invisible de l'espace, avec des chants brûlés
Dans les royaumes de l'inouï créé de lointains
Paysages, exaltés et profonds.

Misterioso

Il se hâte vers sa fin, le requiem
Que des événements inconnus doivent interrompre;
Prémonitoires de la rupture les cordes forcées
A travers tous les tons par le vent rude
De l'angoisse! et répétition de pressentiments
Intérieurs: ces fusées d'étoiles rouges et
L'Etoile de la Mort au milieu qui projette

Sur nous la paralysie de ses rayons pénétrants
Jusqu'au recoin le plus secret de l'âme,
Là où coupable le miroir tourne
Sans cesse et ne cesse pas de rendre
Des images deformées de notre détresse: telle la fumée
Qui accompagne la Bête hors de l'abîme, l'agneau
Meurtri, et ces chevaliers aux quatre couleurs criantes . . .

Mais toutes les visions surgies hors du temps
Se fanent enfin; ne peuvent nullement cacher
La révélation de la nudité affreuse
De l'homme tragique divisé en lui-même
Qui maintenant doit monter sur l'échafaud de son trône
Et porter une couronne de feu, et être trahi, tomber
Dans les ténèbres du mythe pour retrouver son Christ.

Epilogue: 1939

Les vrais témoins ne sont plus aujourd'hui
Ecoutés, le silence les cache
(En était un celui qu'on commémore
Ici: en exil son esprit,
Sa ville natale perdue
Aux barbares bruns et noirs, et ses partitions
Verboten comme un scandale dangereux).

Villes glorieuses de la musique, de l'art,
Vienne, Salzburg et Prague, des millepieds
Chaussés de fer ont envahi vos rues,
L'araignée hideuse de la croix gammée
Partout suspend ses toiles; ce sont des rats
Qui font la musique de chambre dans vos chambres;
Et dans vos jardins ombrageux se cachent les loups.

Elle s'agrandit toujours la tache
Flagrante, et déshonore l'histoire.
Les injustes règnent, leurs orateurs perfides
Rendent sourd le peuple tandis que tombent les haches.
Mais hors de l'avenir quel orage effrayant
Va effacer leurs dernières traces avec ses foudres!
Les vrais témoins nous resteront toujours.

Été 1939

Woman and Earth

Kingdom Come, Vol. 3, No. 9 (Nov.–Dec. 1941)

Was stronger than the light this heart which was in her
Her blood more open to the influence of the moon
Than blood outspread, her night more dark and hirsute
      than
The night and just as spark[l]ing and as hard
A sex more than a soul a star more than a sex
A temple with hair hanging from the roof

And sleeping are that other granite, roses long-preserved
Which pass and disappear into the light's pure bath
Weakness unfelt and distance unperceived
O lofty lands and foreign azure sky

Weigh on her now who is no more
A breast or tears or shuddering in time
Who has turned round beneath the earth
To face another and more ashen sun.

New Directions, Vol.7 (1942)

This heart was while she lived more hard than light
Beneath the influence of the moon her life-blood lay
More openly than spilt blood spread; her night
Was darker and more hirsute than the night, but just as
Sparkling and as hard: more sex than soul, more star
Than sex: a temple with hair flowing from the roof

And you who sleep! Strange granite and rich roses
      decomposed
Passing away and vanishing as in a bath of
Purest light: weakness unfelt and distance

unperceived –
O lofty lands and foreign azure sky

Weigh down on her who is in Time no more
A breast nor quivering nor tears
Who has turned round beneath the earth
To face another and more ashen sun.

Poems 1937–42 (1943)

Was stronger than the light this heart which beat in her
Her blood to the moon's influence more open lay
Than lifeblood shed; her night was denser and more
       hirsute than
The Night, and just as sparkling and as hard -
More sex than soul a star more than a sex
Temple with tresses drifting from the dome

Are sleeping now that other granite, roses overblown
That pass away and vanish in the light's pure lake -
Old weaknesses felt no more, all distance done away:
O lofty lofty lands and alien azure sky
Weigh down on her who now is no more known
As bosom or as spasm or as hot tears spilt in Time:
Who underneath the ground has turned right round
To face another, a more ashen sun.

The Two Witnesses
New Directions, Vol. 7 (1942)

Have mercy cruel Lamb upon these last two witnesses
Who shall be slain in the red cloak and have no resting-
        place
And take O Liberty their gory carcasses in care
For these are the two candlebearers of the Lord
For they have had the power to lock the sky
For their mouths' fire consumes the unjust man
For they have changed the waters into blood
But in the end the dread Beast of the pit
Has been sent power to deliver them
Has declared war and slain them and left them undone.

Poems 1937–42 (1943)

Have pity, O harsh Lamb upon these last two
Witnesses who shall in scarlet cloak be slain and have no
        tomb
And take O Liberty into thy charge their red remains
For these are the two holy candle-bearers of the Lord
For they have been given power to shut the sky
For their mouths' fire has quite consumed the unjust man
For they have turned the waters into blood
But at last the Beast of the abyss
Has been sent power to deliver them
Has made war and has killed them and all their deeds has
        undone

Post Mortem

O mercury-green glare, grey flesh, black hair,
Harsh, frigid spasm, the spilt pool and spreading stain,
Mixed in the spirit, sharply printed there
By nightly pressures, between web-like sheets,
Such horrifying sheets as cling in dreams:
How can timebound a memory escape
From so much detritus
And humus of the depths?
Yet the bespittled hidden face,
Vile and reviled
Emerges out of life as from a sleep,
The complex hatred and long-implicating lie
At last released that heavy skein unwound.

[Autumn 1937, revised Summer 1940]

21 Grove Terrace
Teddington
Middlesex
31.III.39

Dear Mr. Dickins,

Thank you again for the proofs, returned herewith, and for your note. The poems 'De Profundis' and 'Lachrymae' are <u>not</u> translations; the ms which Fabers sent you ought to contain the French text of <u>four</u> poems by Pierre Jean Jouve together with my translations of them, nos. 2 and 3 being entitled 'In Insula Monti Majoris' and 'Interior Landscape', the others without titles; the poems of mine must have been enclosed by mistake. Eliot's intention was to publish the French originals with their translation opposite, but I do not suppose you will have enough space at your disposal to be able to do this?

I very much liked the first number of *Poetry* [London], and particularly the Editorial, the point of view of which I am completely in sympathy with. It represents a very welcome change from the bad-tempered, superior, carping tone used by most of the intellectual periodicals nowadays.

Now that I am living in England again, I hope I may be able to meet you some time and discuss poetry and so on.

Yours sincerely,
David Gascoyne

21 Grove Terrace
Teddington
Middlesex
8.V.39

Dear Tambi,

Here is the revised version which I have just completed of a long poem I first wrote three years ago. Could it go into your May issue, do you think? I would very much like to see it printed now. (I also send a brief note a propos the poem which you might or might not care to use.

I am sorry not to have been able to send you the Jouve translations yet, but I've just come back from a week at George Barker's in the country and have not had time to rewrite them. Couldn't you ask *The Criterion* to see if they can't find the original copy?

Shall be seeing you soon again, I hope –

Yours sincerely,
David Gascoyne

Yes, You!

Stealthy and utterly vain, insane
small nagging voice,
You go on and on, and on, repeating
your wretched obstinate
Unforgivable lies,
Your impotent, impudent accusations,
Your little nastinesses and
your filthy imaginings,
On, and on, and on,
Dogged enemy of all truth, and
beauty, and courage of the mind,
and honesty, and the will to
change, and the power to love,
You go on and on with your
stealthy whispering and your
guilty prudent repetition,
Because you are the contemptible
powerless victim
Of a blind raging power by
which you are possessed,
And you go on and on because you
could not even if you would, know
how to stop,
And perhaps in reality, you are
not utterly guilty in the end,
Because you are quite unconscious
of what you are doing, of what
you keep having to say
Over and over and over again,
And quite unconscious of whose
victim it is you are.
Be assured that the silence which
Preceded and follows you is overwhelmingly
vast and deep and just.

[Notebook, *c.* 1950]

Untitled

Yes. Thank you. Now I can start the day
Writing this poem. You have shown me the way
I have no longer any gift to give
Yet I must it seems write poems, one has to live.
For a long while I've been piling up a lot
Of things I badly wanted to say but could not.
I've lost my sense of form, I have no style.
No nostalgic melody, no magic, only bile.

[Notebook III, 1950]

Letters from Pierre Jean Jouve to David Gascoyne

Cher David,   14 décembre 1956
J'espère que vous no partirez pas sans venir nous dire au revoir. Je dois aussi vous recommander de me rendre la copie de *Macbeth* que je vous ai donnée, et vous devinez quel intérêt j'attache a votre jugement sur ce lourd travail.

      Je vous embrasse,
            Pierre Jean Jouve

Cher David,   5 février 1957
Je ne sais pas que vous ayez ce portrait – du moins dans ce format. Je vous l'offre en remerciement de votre amitié si fidèle, et de beaucoup de choses – comme cette excellente notice du *London Magazine*.

      Je vous embrasse,
            Pierre

Letters from Blanche Reverchon-Jouve to David Gascoyne.[36]

7 rue A.-Chantin
Mon ami, votre lettre m'a
paru merveilleuse et m'a
donné le plus grand désir
de vous voir – Mais où et
comment?
Ecrivez-moi encore –
Votre BR Jouve

Mon cher ami,   7 août
On a écrit que ces temps vécus avaient été les temps
dédiés aux poètes – je crois surtout qu'ils ont été les
temps où 'les âmes des poètes' (Dieu seul sait ce que
cela veut dire) ont été le plus durement bombardées –

Pierre et moi seront à Paris a la fin de Septembre –
J'espère que vous nous y rejoindrez bientôt – Peter
Watson que nous avons vu à Genève nous aidera
certainement à faire ce qu'il faut pour cela –
À vous de tout coeur
BR Jouve

---

36 In marked contrast to her husband's meticulous handwriting Blanche's,
on the evidence here of the note and the letter, sprawled large and clumsily
across the page with an average of four words to the line. The letter itself
comprises two pages. I am very grateful to Dr Richard Lund of Northumbria
University who helped me decipher several of the words.

A NEW POEM BY PIERRE JEAN JOUVE: 'LANGUAGE' [37]

Last spring, the *Mercure de France* published a new book of poetry by Pierre Jean Jouve: *Langue*, the fifth volume of his poetic work to have appeared since the end of the war. In the four previous volumes (*Hymne, Génie, Diadème,* and *Ode*), Jouve's poetic style has been seen to undergo a process of modification and renewal; the style of *Ode* was quite unlike that of anything that he had written earlier, while *Langue*, which is in a style that seems closely to resemble it, represents a still further phase of evolution, corresponding to the inner development of the poet in his struggle for spiritual significance.

It has been apparent for some time that the whole poetic work of Pierre Jean Jouve will eventually reveal itself to be constructed according to a consciously conceived plan. With the publication last year of the autobiographical commentary on his own writings called *En Miroir* (extracts from which appeared simultaneously in three different revues last February) and the broadcasting of a series of ten *entretiens* by the French radio last autumn, the monumental outlines of the structure which his work as a whole represents may become more easily distinguishable. In its entirety this work will soon consist of at least a dozen volumes of poetry, four volumes of prose fiction (all predating 1935), and five or six volumes of essays.

In *En Miroir*, Jouve has written: 'My passion becomes involved only when confronted with an idea, a scheme, that is at once the same, and different.' There are a number of themes that are fundamental and recurrent throughout his entire production, and one may be sure that, however unfamiliar the style and imagery of his most recent poetry, most of these themes will be found to recur, though possibly in transmuted or augmented form, in the poems of the sequence called *Langue*. It contains altogether forty-one poems, and is divided into

37 *London Magazine*, Vol. 2, No. 2 (February 1955), pp. 49–52.

three main sections. The dominant theme may be defined as the *a priori* non-existence of a language in which the unknown may be expressed, and the struggle to create, which is at the same time the prayer to be granted, such a language; and thus we may say that the work has a certain essential similarity to Eliot's *Four Quartets*, although the latter is in most ways so very different in conception and style.

One of the most characteristic features of Pierre Jean Jouve both as a novelist and as a poet has always been his highly developed aware-ness of the Unconscious, of the guilt by which the Unconscious is dominated in all men, and of the struggle in the Unconscious of the instincts of life and death, which seem always to be locked inextrica-bly together. Poetry, like the works of the great mystics, Jouve regards as proceeding from Eros, or rather, as representing the highest degree of sublimation of the erotic instinct (speaking, in the preface to *Sueur de sang*, for instance, of 'l'élévation à des substances si profondes, ou si élévées, qui dérivent de la pauvre, de la belle puissance érotique humaine'). In *Langue*, it is clear that what the poet is attempting is above all the conjuration of a new transport of sublimation by means of which erotic energy may be transformed into the power to give reality through articulation in language to a hitherto unknown spiri-tual dimension.

> Mais que baise, une seule fois, mon âme nue sur mon âme!
> Innovant les mondes nouveaux.

At the same time, the poem is philosophical in the specifically Socratic sense of being a meditation directed towards 'preparation in view of death'. An experience of the approach of death, and of an Orphic reconciliation with death resulting in a restoration to life of the loved one, is embodied in the substance of the poem, and it is this which provides the subject of what are certainly the most beautiful and most deeply moving pages of the whole text, in the passage which begins: 'Alors arriva d'un coup la face du Tonnerre.'

In the concluding poems of the sequence, the poet's voice attains to a tranquillity beyond desolation, and the principal theme of the whole is clarified in a last statement which is like the resolution at the end of a musical composition (the music-like structure of the work is another feature which it shares with the *Four Quartets*). The following in particular provides a key to the whole intention of *Langue*.

> At so many years' distance from the day of birth, with death distant by only a few days, after so many figures that appeared to rise and fall in the same sky of desire wherein disappointment and pleasure were both of the same shade of blue,
>
> after all the monotony befallen in the gardens – the distance that seemed so close at hand yet so remotely lost – and all the insecurity of the end – art in its repetitions altogether terrified to be alone amidst unbounded and bare space,
>
> one seeks the meaning and the letter and the spirit: the meaning is dear to God: the meaning is what reaches the God-consciousness, and as a phrase resounds from the main vocable and rings through all the rest that are disposed on either side of it,
>
> the word of life is only to be read in the absurd – imprinted within absolute Absurdity and shining there like love of which the forms are infinite.

At the present time it is reassuring to find that there can still exist in the world some poets entirely preoccupied, not with an art of agreeable diversion, but with an art that bears witness to the life of the spirit beyond and out of death.

The part of the poem quoted above is not a particularly difficult passage to render into English; but a good deal of *Langue* presents the translator with problems of almost insuperable difficulty. Solemnity of tone does not ever pass easily from one language into another; and invocation and apostrophe are apt to sound impossibly odd in translation. The following three poems, or subsections of the poem, happen to seem to lend themselves more readily than most of the rest of the text to recreation or transcription in an idiom which it is hoped is not too unlike either the poetic style of the original, or readable English.

I

During that moulting season of the formless final world

The conquerors held out still: alone and without horses either of plaster or of gold

And without money (lost in the sands and in the circuses, and on all fronts)

Without even a moist lance's oriflamme. And then what thrusts of troops that never moved!

Pure conquerors of ancient time – and all cathedrals in their train –

They awaited with their passion in the swarming towns of dwarfs

An extraordinary onslaught of empty emotion and explosiveness

Which might enable all to be recovered by the vitals that were losing all their blood.

II

Ah! the poet now writes only for the heavens' empty space

Pure blue that winter can no longer see! he writes in conjuration of the silence of the snows

Of the stifling of fallacious festal days! and in the lack and in the lacklustre it reveals, each line he writes is just as though he were not there (and his slim figure, dressed in the lights' glare, is just as though he were not there),

And in his solitude devoted to that admirable, secret conjuration, behold him pleading his peculiar loves

When none would undertake to risk love's courage in his stead:

Then on the fabled winds' black shore, over the seaweeds' slumber, under nearly weightless whirling swells of fog,

He seals the word up in the bottle of green glass,

Bells of despair and horrible seawrack!

He launches on the highest wave a bottle without action, force or aim, yet which one day

The waves will wash up to love's level, beyond beauty, beyond glory, beyond day.

III

Clear light of day! flow once more through the furrow you have
worn upon the mortal avenues

Gleam on the capitals and globes of stone, waken the sacred snakes,

All men's activities! And mortal thought of mine pursue once more

Your way towards hope's narrow zone, with great deliberate works
in view:

Both works and death before my eyes stand like glad monuments
devoured by the sky's plants,

Pure ruin well contented to be filled with its vast future and its
natural love.

APPENDIX B
FACSIMILES: letters, handwritten draft translations and copies

B1 *Pieta*: draft translation of poem by Jouve

B2 'Helen's sweet laughter': draft translation of poem by Jouve

B3 *To Himself*: draft translation of poem by Jouve

B4 *P*: draft translation of poem by Jouve

B5 *Tempo di Mozart*: draft translation of poem by Jouve

B6 'Green is the windswept plain': draft translation of poem by Jouve

B7 'Green waters! If the rocks tumble…': draft translation of poem by Jouve

B8 *Rabbouni*: draft translation of poem by Jouve

B9 'Solitude has its own strange way': draft translation of poem by Jouve

B10 'What does the dragon want?': draft translation of poem by Jouve

B11 'Beneath the great spread table…': draft translation of poem by Jouve

B12 'Hear how on the wind that ruffles…': draft translation of poem by Jouve

B13 *Dernier Signe à Salzbourg*: handwritten copy of poem by Jouve

B14 'Untitled Mozart poem': draft translation of poem by Jouve

B15 'O joie de tant d'années': handwritten copy of poem by Jouve

B15 *Sanctus à Salzbourg*: handwritten copy of poem by Jouve

B16 'O joy of so many years': draft translation of poem by Jouve

B16 'O terribly dark master…': draft translation of poem by Jouve (fragment)

B17 'Jouve on [Alban] Berg': draft translation of essay by Jouve (fragment)

B18 Gascoyne on the twelfth volume of Jouve's poetic works (fragment)

B19 'Pierre Jean Jouve. Those who today…': (prose fragment)

B20 Letter from Gascoyne to Anthony Dickins at *Poetry* (London): 31 March 1939

B21 Letter from Gascoyne to Tambimuttu at *Poetry* (London): 8 May 1939

B22 Letter from Gascoyne to Tambimuttu at *Poetry* (London): 24 November 1940

B23 Letter from Tambimuttu at *Poetry* (London) to Gascoyne: 11 June 1945

B24 Letter from Pierre Jean Jouve to Gascoyne: 14 December 1956

B25 Letter from Pierre Jean Jouve to Gascoyne: 5 February 1957

B26 Letter from Blanche Reverchon Jouve to Gascoyne: no date (?1947)

Pieta

P. T. Towne.

Maternal shadow, closely to you ~~do you~~ hold
His dying body on the brinks of madness.
Hold
Him to you close. To see him still means ah!
what rending shreds
Of sacred horror ~~binding your~~ ~~weak~~ softness round
with love

O memory
~~Mindful~~
~~Mindful~~ how starkly ~~that~~ you were destitute ~~years ago~~
And mindful of how his body out of yours,
~~That beauty~~ Once born forth, that body's soul,
was when ~~the~~ back fires
split ~~the~~ across your brow.

(fragment)

JOUVE.

Helen's sweet laughter pierces the panes to reach
The solid wall upon the heights; and the cold lakes
Weep joyful tears for a hundred acts of love and stars
Of transport and desire over those most strange plants
Sent here in memory of her, at the pure hour
When warming ~~underneath~~ the ~~velvet~~ sensual velvet
            of another sky
Aurora combing her gold hair Beckoned her ~~who~~
                    towards death.

                from "Génie"

To Himself

Write now ~~for~~ only the sky

Write for the curved arc ~~of the~~

~~And let~~ to no black letter of lead

    ~~letter black with lead~~

Resort to wrap thy writing in

Write for the odour and the breath

Write for the sheet of silver leaf

Let no ~~unglorious~~ human face

Have glimpse or knowledge or rumour thereof

Write for the god and for the fire

Write for the sake of a desired

And may nothing to do with man ~~place~~ intrude

P

When I was born appeared this strange
"That" now I keep on seeing under every
downcast sky
The swaddling-clothes that I divided at
Was stamped my Earth
on the right hand with
shadow marks that spot
The words Welcome
And upon the left appeared the letter
Stands for Pity for P
(on us all) towards everyone.

P. T. Jones.

PIERRE JEAN JOUVE

TEMPO DI MOZART
(from "Matière Céleste")
1956/7

The sky the vast sky is of wind and of stone   [breath?]
Stone of azure hardui and trembl: air of rock
What still sings in the ancient violins
How caressing are the hearts of the grass genius

How precious is the stone with the months of ash
How pure(it is)! Seasonless, the gold's volume   [unseasonable]
~~What~~ How cold the ardour in its folds
Inviolable hymen of the day

The earth would thrust its breast into justice
The azure, azure, azure! would perish tender and blue.

But the hour just as in a drama of forces interchanged   [into]
Like ~~a violating love of~~ virgin mother's violating love
Like the poisonous flesh of flowers   [rich]
Or great as Christ's passion in the dark   [was]
Has changed.

Heavenly hurricane held back by an edge
The void is hung on the edge of your eyes
Male hurricane! All is lost, all is calm
Of the world made by the hatred of your eyes
All is white all is dying but dazzling bright
With what is (passing reborn) crossing the suffering of your eyes
All collapses into naked springs of tears
Falls silent, and in the silence angels keep
The most precious pale surrender is fulfilled

I am he who loves
Child whose swaddling clothes are now ~~thrown~~ spread out
In clouds in ~~their~~ insights of reason and prayers
Child whose eyes were pierced by rays
Child of enormous wrath
While ~~my man's eyes were~~ I was shutting my ~~child grown~~ man's eyes.

JOVE

Green is the waveswept plain at the hour of
the budding
corn
Green are the windswept trees, green is
the breeze
the thoughtful slope
Green is the sleeping wood that winds across the
scene
Green is the ditches, and the soul. O vast scope
of my eyes

Green and the grey of ... and the limpid wrath
Of the sky above, and the gentle kindness quiet
The rooks fly off
move away towards the stern
horizon's rim
Where presently the huge smokes of the city shall
appear

Green waters! if the rocks tumble ~~down in tragedy~~ tragically down
In harmony with the return of love's embrace
With darkness and if the weather gives a
                              sparce ~~blood~~ wood
With feathers and with acid; and the antique
                              light
To see the wandering weightless cumulus clouds
With the irritating crushers ~~~~ Begins to laugh;
And° then the grass fringe ~~around the waters~~ pools
        edge is blown back leaving it bare

And ~~the~~ nymph ~~in~~ whose eyes reflected ~~his~~
        love paradise ~~replied~~:
"~~Bsarow Rather~~ see here how in the distant
                              gulley rise
Enormous silvered masses overshadowing the trees
The blood of the ~~hardy~~ jagged-shadowed valley that
        the panther haunts
The ~~rock falls that torment the ~~masons'~~
                      ~~forshaped yard~~
And in ~~their~~ souls the wounded warriors ~~remnt~~
~~The Dismayed~~ love dying in a naked ~~bronty's~~
                      nest

Rabbouni.

And Christ appeared to ~~the~~ Mary in the
        guise
Of a gardener, ~~bent as over a bed~~.
        She just then saw
The empty tomb in which angels or
        shades
Seemed like her grief as dusky as that
      shrine ~~those~~

And with her tears still dripping from
     her cheeks upon her breast
           was struck by
Just then her glistening eye ~~caught~~ a
       man's form
" Where hast thou laid him, gardener," she
             asked
" That I may go and bring back his remains

And lay them here again?" And the man
                           spoke but one word
Mary, so far-away so broken and so robbed
                              of life
That she dropped to the ground and ~~they~~ heard
                          him say
But do not touch me. Master! O Rabboni!

Jouve

The Glorious Cross.

The cross he bears in this
Is of the lightest iron inscribed

Solitude has its own strange way
Of mirroring as in a frozen marsh
The defeat passing out of victory
The doubt on bleeding thigh
clearly disclosed

And strange proliferating seedy grass
Batrachian blue or spiny cactuses
Vivid rose leaning towards the dahlias
met
In the glare of the massive, nude and
stupefying sun

And countless anxious pangs that
matter (Nature) feels;
Devoured by insects pious hordes
The calcined fibres: (the) tranquil, destitute
Is death's slow last extremity in this
abandoned place.

What does the dragon want? that I be fond of him
His moving is around about the sky
Within the bowls ~~most~~ furthermost depths
With all his ~~thousandfold~~ thousandfold ancient degrees

His tears his hesitating stays
And his red mouths of flame
And it is not till he has uttered I
Want to the cloudy dark, the mire, the shame

And ~~is~~ not till he has said I am
Out of his eyes that ~~look like~~ an old crook
"That wisdom has no ~~longer~~ any ~~things~~
(regal tears)

Against ~~it~~ haggard kindliness

But it is when he cries I am ashamed
(The tears the hesitating stays)
That man goes rushing back to any shame
To give his passion its old sway again.

Pierre Jean Jouve.

Ode.

Trombes — Nef — Nuits.

I.

Beneath the great spread table of the
sea the wornout ~~hills of~~ *hills* ~~withy~~ "trombes"
~~Are~~ repeated by *the* grief and the green
                                    misty embraces

Of the breasts full of male power in
the black and diamondstudded sky;
Aluck-a-day! and well-a-day! and the
etherized thunderbolts of morn

Wounding wound of ~~the~~ eye, ~~holds~~ the
                                    ~~thick scrabbling~~
Round ~~the~~ circuit, funereal pictures,
                        Of ~~two~~ diamondstudded eagles.

P. N. Tower

Hear how on the wind that ruffles the
Striped fleece of thinnest cloud
Comes the song of the nightingale or Queen
of the night
her throat
salty roses from the
slowly blackness the cry
Of the nocturnal jasmin and the purplish
Of the secretly creatures of the shades tuted skin
: night
murder
And the stars slow solemny afterwards.
night blood
Hear the fierce trills of the churning
queen of death
Triumphantly break into small sliming spots
across the slumberer's
wake

Pierre Jean JOUVE

Dernier Signe à Salzbourg

Ame et château soleil pesant et purs montagnes antiques
Génie et gloire et vous oubli de mon maître
Musique insaisissable en des frayeurs de Christ
Repos et vues ! imagination de retour.

Et si ta mort avec ses vêtements de soie
Que prépare le temps de demain se détourne ?
Qu'elle te voie plein de larmes lucide
Voir l'injuste monter sur les terres humides
Courber l'homme et défaire son âme de couleur
Car absous sera le coupable ainsi qu'il est dit
Et sous le signe du soleil de diable il renouvera
Les prisons aux yeux clairs
Du gémissement de ce que fut l'homme et soi

---

2) How precious in the rock with
                    its mounds of ash
How pure and out of season
           the great mass of
their chilly feel the   gold !
                    ardour of it a
                              foes
Of the inviolable regimen of the
                    the it day.

PIERRE JEAN JOUVE

Untitled Mozart Poem (date?)

How the sky, the vast sky is
breaks full of ~~~~ of wind and rock
O harden the ~~~~ rock, and make
the rock's air shake
How steely sounds the singing of
the antique violins' strings.
How pure and out of season seems
the great mass of gold!
How chilly feels the ardour in the
the fields
Of the inviolable hymns of the day.

¶ Here the sky, the vast sky is full of
breath of air and rock
O harden the pure rock and cause to
shiver the rock's air
How steely sounds the singing of the
antique violins' strings
How gentle feels the stroking of
the green ~~~~ heart

Pierre Jean JOUVE

C'est beaucoup plus qu'un
prince, car c'est un homme
Sarastre dans La Flûte enchantée

Ô pie de tant d'années ! et toi flûte enchantée
Résonne encore un jour sur le flot du mystère
Baigne l'amour premier
Donne-nous la promesse
Hors des tombes d'église
Fais flamber en riant ces vieux rituels noirs
Mais guéris-nous du fer et des vives matières
Qui surgit d'un horizon mort l'amour premier

Sanctus à Salzbourg

Ô maître terriblement noir de l'aventure
Vague feuille de l'été retombée
Sur la mémoire de mes morts camarades
Éclaire sans fin sculpture et cimetière
Ô maître terriblement vrai de mon aventure
Soupir inlassable de lumière
Masse des chœurs masse du ciel d'été
Masse des portes sans portes et sans clés,
Ô maître du néant sieur de l'aventure
Suppression des poitrines tendres et des maisons
Suppression des chœurs des absolutions
Angoisse de la vie de Dieu de la nature

He is far more than a
prince, for he's a man

O joy of so many years! and O magic flute
Re-echo one day upon the secret stage
[illegible] Barbs / Cleanses the [illegible] love
[illegible] up the Hedge
Out of the church [illegible]
Make those of old black rituals laughing [illegible]
But over us of the [illegible] and of the [illegible] substances
Which with a dead [illegible] conceal the [illegible] la[illegible]

---

(2)

O terribly dark master of the dead / earthbound
Magic leaf of summer [illegible] Bach
On the [illegible] of my corroded defeated
Smile without end [illegible] sceptres and [illegible]
O terribly brave master of my [illegible]
[illegible] spirit's tireless smile
Mass of choirs mass of the summer day
Mass of
Men of

Jouve on Berg.

The Concerto has two parts, which are divided into several lesser ~~parts~~ inter-linked ~~sections~~ It begins (Andante - Introduction) with a most strange undulating movement, a series of fifths based on the four notes of the ~~~~ cordes vides of the violin, which in becoming ~~~~ reengendered in multiple fashion in every register of the orchestra, ~~~~ and so ~~~~ acquiring an impressive density, ~~expresses~~ most wonderfully a predestined grace, ~~~~ nervously alert and open ~~~~ upwards to the ~~showering~~ ~~~~ of favours ~~falling down across from heaven~~ so as to a ~~gradually~~ ~~~~ efflorescence of Danaëan gold.

Pierre Jean Jouve.

In February 1956, Jouve published the 12th volume of his poetic works. Four sections, seven suites of poems. Phénix, Fortune, Jeune Fille, Tombeau de Berg, Élégie, untitled suite, Invention sur un Thème.

Jeune Fille is a poem that recreates in words the Violin Concerto of Alban Berg (premonition of his own death, becoming now almost his sole theme) and contains a quotation of the first two bars of the second movement of Berg's Lyric Suite.

The theme of the "Invention" is Le mystère engendrant la conscience de l'art.

Pierre Jean Jouve. Those who today are able to recognize in Jouve the most important poet at present writing in France, may well be proud. That he is this is objectively deduced from a just appreciation of the veritable content of his writings: I am thinking now of "Langue" — particularly p. 63. Here is uncontrovertably formulated an instance of the maximum function that poetry can now perform.

Jouve cannot always recognize himself speaking in what he has written. Another voice, the Other Voice, ventriloquizes through him. He is capable of allowing the subliminal message to inscribe itself at the heart of his poetry in this way, because of the long utterly disinterested toil which he has devoted to the perfecting of a technique of imaginatively transcendental discursivity, (his intention meanwhile often seeming preoccupied with private aesthetic-erotic antisatisfaction).

21, Grove Terrace,
Teddington,
Middlesex.

31·III·39

Dear Mr. Dickins,

    Thank you for the proofs, returned herewith, and for your note. The poems "De Profundis" and "Lachrymae" are _not_ translations; the ms which Fabers sent you ought to contain the French text of _four_ poems by Pierre Jean Jouve together with my translations of them, nos. 2 and 3 being entitled "In Insula Monti Majoris" and "Interior Landscape," the others without titles; the poems of mine must have been enclosed by mistake. Eliot's intention was to publish the French originals with their translation opposite, but I do not suppose you will have enough space at your disposal to be able to do this?

    I very much liked the first number of "Poetry", and particularly the Editorial, the point of view of which I am completely in sympathy with. It represents a very welcome change from the bad-tempered, superior, carping tone used by most of the intellectual periodicals nowadays.

    Now that I am living in England again, I hope I may be able to meet you some time and discuss poetry and so on. Yours sincerely,
David Gascoyne.

21, Grove Terrace,
Teddington,
Middlesex.
8·V·39

Dear Tambi,

Here is the revised version which I
have just completed of a long poem I first
wrote three years ago. Could it go into your
May issue, do you think? I should very much
like to see it printed now. (I also send a
brief note a propos the poem which you might
or might not care to use).

I am sorry not to have been able to
send you the Jouve translations yet, but I've
just come back from a week at George Barker's
in the country and have not had time to
rewrite them. Couldn't you ask the "Criterion"
to see if they can't find the original copy?

Shall be seeing you soon again, I
hope —

Yours sincerely,
David Gascoyne

21, Grove Terrace,
Teddington, Middlesex.
24.XI.40.

Dear Tambi,
    I have the pleasure of sending you a
translation I have just done of an essay of Jouve's
which seems to me to be very much up your present
street. I very much hope that you will like it well
enough, and find it sufficiently relevant to the ideas
you are now engaged in putting across, to include it
in your next number. It's an essay I've vaguely
been meaning to translate ever since I first read it
about three years ago — at which time it helped me
considerably to clarify several problems which were

2.

then bothering me about my own writing —; and then, after
our last conversation about possible material for "Poetry,"
it suddenly occurred to me that it was probably just
the sort of thing you wanted, and I sat down and
started the English version right away. (If the style
seems a bit heavily baroque, I must explain that, if
anything, the original French is more so; though personally,
I don't like it any the less for that.)
    I'm also sending you an article on Kenneth Patchen,
whom I believe I mentioned to you the other day. I'm
afraid it's a bit rambling and stodgy; but if there was
anything in it you liked, perhaps it could be pruned to
a more suitable length. Are you intending to use

the Hart Crane article some time, by the way?

Next, I'm going to try a short "review" of the new Brokosch poems, which don't over-excite me but which seem to provide an opportunity for making a pregnant remark or two. I also want to write a series of short, loosely-connected general notes on the present condition and future possibilities of modern poetry, — that is, if my present comparatively productive mood lasts long enough to survive interruptions...

Do let me hear from you soon about this and that.

With love, yrs.

David.

Poetry London

EDITED BY TAMBIMUTTU
26 *Manchester Square*, *London W*1; *WEL* 8178

11th June, 1945.

David Gascoyne, Esq.,
c/o N. Croziere, Esq.,
31, Downside Crescent,
N.W. 3.

My dear David,

You should be receiving a cheque for £20 in the course of the next few days. I have also written to my friend, Dr. Wells, who is a painter and sculptor as well as a good surgeon, of the Scilly Isles, and I hope he will be able to fix you up with a two months' holiday in a quiet farmhouse. We shall pay all expenses for two months and I hope during that time you will be able to complete some of the books that we have commissioned from you - for example, Pierre Jean Jouve translations.

If you have the time, do drop in sometime this week.

Love,
Tambi

14 décembre 1964

Cher David,

J'espère que vous ne m'en voulez pas d'avoir venu nous dire au revoir. Je nous admirons vous et coopération que je souhaite que vous m'donner. Je rendre la copie de *Macbeth* que je vous m'donner et s'ennuie de vous devinez quant insiste! J'attache à robe Jugement es vous devinez quant insiste! J'attache à robe Jugement es ce lourd Devait.

Je vous embrasse.

Pierre de Tort Cacile

7, Rue Antoine Chantin
5 février 1957.

Cher David,

Je ne vous [...] que vous me [...] que j'ai [...] et je ne [...] de [...] en effet, vous [...] de [...] vous avez [...] [...] votre excellente notice en [...] française.

Je vous embrasse.

Pierre

7. rue d. Chaseloir

Cher ami, votre lettre m'a
bien merveilleuse & m'a
donné le plus grand désir
de vous voir — mais où &
comment ?

Écrivez-moi encore —

votre B. Constant —